DIVER'S ALMANAC

Guide to the Hawaiian Islands

By Rick Baker

Author
Rick Baker

Editor
Pat Brumm

Medical Editor
David Boaz, M.D.

Contributing Editors
Cory Gray
Judi Alves-Jurewitz

Graphic Designer
Laurel Shelton

Typesetting
Holly Woodard

Cover Photos
Rick Baker
David McCray
Hawaii Visitor Bureau

Watercolor Maps
Laurel Shelton

Production
RH Communications, Inc.

Publisher
Triton Publishing
P.O. Box 3486
Palos Verdes, CA 90274

About The Author

Rick Baker is a writer/photographer who makes his home in Huntington Beach, California. A graduate of San Jose State University, he majored in Marine Geology and Chemistry. In his column called Oceans in *Pacific Diver Magazine*, he explores the environmental challenges we face today in our oceans. He also teaches Oceanography and Marine Geology at the Orange County Marine Institute at Dana Point, California.

He is presently publisher of *The Coastal Monitor*, the *Journal of the Oceanic Society*. This journal promotes programs designed to monitor environmental changes in the marine environment. He has also recently revised and updated the book, *Diver's Almanac: Guide to the West Coast*, edited *Diver's Almanac: Guide to Florida & the Keys* and is co-author of *The California Dive Boat Book*.

Acknowledgments

I thank all the dive shop managers, dive guides, photographers, artists and tourist board representatives who supplied so much of the information and talent needed to create this almanac.

Contributing Photographers

Rick Baker
P.O. Box 6218
Huntington Beach, CA 92615

Ronald Owen
P.O. Box 4277
Napa, CA 94558
(707) 226-2325

David McCray
4248 Via Pinzon
Palos Verdes Estates, CA 90274

Cory Gray
5319 Reynier Avenue
Los Angeles, CA 90056
(213) 437-6468

Bill Shofstall
810 Huntington St.
Huntington Beach, CA 92648
(714) 536-8910

Hawaii Visitor Bureau
3440 Wilshire Blvd. Suite 402
Los Angeles, CA 90010

DIVER'S ALMANAC

Guide to the Hawaiian Islands

TABLE OF CONTENTS

PART VI – DIVING SAFETY & MEDICINE

A great deal of effort has been made to obtain accurate information for this publication. The information was obtained from numerous sources. Due to the sheer magnitude of the task, not all of the information presented herein has been confirmed, but has been accepted as presented by area contacts. For this reason, this book is intended for use as a guide only. Additional information should be obtained for areas visited. The editors and publishers assume no liability for its use, and encourage caution and prudence in application of information presented. Remember, diving is an inherently dangerous sport.

Photo courtesy of Rick Baker

Word Of Caution To The Reader

Webster defines an almanac as "a publication containing statistical, tabular, and general information." A great deal of effort has been made to obtain accurate information for this publication. Some of it is general, but much of it is statistical, tabular and very specific. No matter how much effort is expended in getting current and accurate information, it is a fact of life that addresses will change and conditions in the sea will vary from year to year and from day to day. Some of this information was obtained from contacts in each area; not all the information was confirmed. General knowledge about scuba diving is constantly changing. For this reason, this book is intended as a guide only. Always contact a local dive shop or dive professional to get current information about the area you are going to dive. The author, editors and publishers assume no liability for its use, and encourage caution and prudence in application of information presented. Remember, diving is an inherently dangerous sport. Skill levels of the dive sites discussed in this book are marked and should be very seriously considered. Remember, if you don't feel comfortable with the dive — don't dive.

Photo courtesy of Cory Gray

Foreword

Each of the Hawaiian Islands is a geographically small, mini continent perched precariously in the middle of the largest and oldest ocean on earth: the Pacific. Start at the southwest corner of any island and trek across the midline toward the northeast corner and you will consistently find the same series of ecological niches. First, you will pass through the dry lee side of the island on your way up to the peak of a volcanic mountain range where temperatures can drop 40 degrees lower than at the coast. As you head over the top and down the northeast or the windward side of the island, you will encounter waterfalls, rivers and a jungle-like terrain. The complexity and diversity of each of these island's ecology matches that of any continent on earth.

Hawaii's underwater world is as complex and diverse as its above-water counterpart. As scuba divers, we have the privilege of experiencing the underwater world as well, which can only enhance our Hawaiian adventure. Every-one who visits Hawaii is aware of the volcanoes pointing skyward, covered with lush vegetation. But as scuba divers, we get a broader view. We can more easily visualize these volcanoes as giant chunks of volcanic rock resting comfortably on the floor of the Pacific Ocean. We can explore the lava tubes where molten rock once flowed into the sea. We can observe coral reefs resting on the flanks of these volcanoes growing ever upward toward the sea's surface as they reach for the sun's light. And to the thousands of species of plants and animals that we can enjoy on land, we add a thousand more that thrive on the sea bottom, some found nowhere else in the world. After a short time, these islands, surrounded by volcanic rocks, take on an unique, multi-dimensional character. To visit and explore these dots of land in the middle of the Pacific deepens one's view of life and of the world.

Although the islands are similar, they are also very different. All the islands are rich in Hawaiian his-tory, yet you will find more muse-ums, sacred heiau and temples on Oahu. All the islands come from volcanic origins, yet on Hawaii you will find the most black, sharp rock, black beaches and volcanoes spewing molten rock. All the islands have a lot of rainfall, yet on Kauai you will find the wettest place on earth, wide rivers, spectacular eroded coastlines and deep cut valleys. All the islands have a rich diversity of plants. Lush jungles accentuated with tall waterfalls provide cover for the windward side, arid dry landscapes expose volcanic rock on the leeward side, and on Maui, on the road to Hana, you will fall in love with the rich assortment of plant life found on this island. You just can't find a vacation spot with more diversity and a greater number of exciting areas to explore on your vacation than the Hawaiian Islands.

Enjoy,
Rick Baker

How to Use This Almanac

This almanac offers a lot of easily accessible information designed to aid the traveling scuba enthusiast in obtaining a most enriching, entertaining, stress-free Hawaiian experience. Each island is described in detail both above and below the water line to help you decide which island or islands best matches your interests. To prepare you for your trip, special reference sections supply some general information on equipment, dive medicine, first aid and safety. In this vein you will also find instructional information on beach, boat, night and wreck diving, so there are no surprises when you finally find yourself on one of the charter boats heading out to Lanai or going night diving off a beach on Maui for the first time. A check list helps you to pack all the right equipment including a first aid kit. A general section on traveling to the islands gets you and your gear on the plane. In addition, a separate "Getting There" segment accompanies each island section to help you get around once you're there.

Once you are there you will need the maps and pertinent information in this almanac to get to the right hotel and figure out the best plan for getting to a dive store, dive boat or a friendly beach for that first dive. Maps guide you through important towns, to the dive operations, dive boats and beaches.

Our "Exploring" section gives you a few days of touring the topside of the islands. Hawaii's rich culture is reflected in its historical museums, ruins and parks. For those who want to experience the great outdoors, a camping and hiking section is also included. Pertinent phone numbers, emergency and tourist information can also be found.

The data in this almanac will give you the know-how you need to manage and enjoy your trip. I hope what you find between these pages will accompany you to the Hawaiian Islands time and time again.

Photo courtesy of Cory Gray

NIIHAU

KAUAI

Princeville
Hanalei
Kokee
Waipouli
Lihue
Airport
Nawiliwili
Poipu

OAHU

Kahuku
Laie
Makaha
Kaneohe
K
Honolulu Airport
Honolulu
Ala Moana
Waikiki
Diamond Head

N

W *E*

S

MOLOKAI

Kalaupapa

Molokai Airport   Halawa

Kaunakakai

Napili

Kapalua West Maui Airport   Wailuku

Kaanapali   Kahului Airport   # MAUI

Lanai Airport   Lanai City   Lahaina

LANAI   Maalaea   Hana

Kihei

Wailea

Makena

KAHOOLAWE

Kawaihae

Kamuela   # HAWAII

Kohala Coast

Waikoloa

Hilo

Keahole Airport   Hilo Airport

Kailua-Kona

Keauhou   Volcano

Punaluu

Naalehu

PART I
Introduction

Historical Hawaii

It is unknown exactly when the Polynesians first found their way to the Hawaiian islands. Some estimates place their arrival at about 750 A.D. but as more archaeological ruins are excavated the further back this historic date is set. Some say the Polynesians arrived at about the time of Christ.

The Polynesians were master sailors and navigators sailing the Pacific without instruments of any kind. Using visual sightings of the sun by day, the moon and stars at night and an instinctual "feel" for the ocean, they navigated with great precision. Studying the wind and wave patterns, the movement of schools of fish and the patterns of clouds in the sky, they piloted their 70 foot long, multi-hulled canoes farther northward reaching points thousands of miles above the equator. A working replica of one of these canoes, the *Hokuleas*, can be found at Pier 7 in downtown Honolulu.

The term Polynesian applies to many tribes from dozens of island groups in the South Pacific. These tribes had some distinct differences in their religious customs and the gods they worshiped but they all had a mastery of the sea. But even with their advanced navigational skills, the journey to the Hawaiian islands to the north was

Square-rigger anchored at Lahaina on Maui. Photo courtesy of Rick Baker

Photo Page 4: Puuhonua O Honaunau National Historical Park on the Big Island of Hawaii. Photo courtesy of Rick Baker

Here at Kealakekua Bay Captain Cook was killed. Photo courtesy of Rick Baker

Historical Hawaii

the upper limit of their navigational expertise.

One tribe, especially known for endurance, lived on one of the harshest, most inhospitable islands in the south Pacific. For this reason, it is thought that the first settlers of Hawaii were from these islands called the Marquesas. The Marquesans were a brutal people. Like many of the Polynesians, the Marquesans practiced human sacrifice but they also had the added distinction of being cannibals.

For a few years after the discovery of these northern islands migration to Hawaii was vigorous. Many traveled back and forth from Polynesia and Hawaii. Then the trips in both direction began to dwindle. For 500 years these early settlers from the Marquesas lived and prospered in Hawaii. Hawaii became isolated. The gentle warm wind, abundant food supply and general calm nature of the islands softened and mellowed this new culture. Cannibalism and human sacrifice slowly died out and a new religion with new gods developed.

For reasons no one understands, the mass migration from Polynesia to Hawaii peaked again around 1300 A.D.. But these new Hawaiians came from Polynesia as conquerors. They quickly took over the islands and changed the culture back to a war-like tribe, reinstated the old gods and human sacrifice. Then it happened again—another 500 years of total isolation. The tribes of the South Pacific totally forgot about the Hawaiian Islands. Trips between Hawaii and the southern islands ceased. The next visitors would be white men. In 1778 it was Captain Cook, the first white man to visit the islands, who spotted Oahu. He decided not to land there, instead sailing north to Waimea on Kauai where he landed to reprovision his ships.

That day would have a tremendous impact on these islands.

Cook left Kauai for the North Pacific and returned a year later finding a safe harbor on the Big Island of Hawaii at Kealakekua Bay. Because of a strange coincidence involving a legend of a Hawaiian God Lono who was said to favor this particular harbor, Cook and his crew were mistaken as gods. The legend even predicted the time of year the god would return and described a vessel that looked much like the square-riggers Cook arrived in. The Hawaiians were euphoric. They offered Cook and his men everything they had and a huge celebration broke out. As would be expected, Cook and his crew took full advantage of the native hospitality, but overstayed their welcome and soon the Hawaiians began to suspect a fraud. Sailing out of the bay, Cook's two sailing ships quickly left the Big Island but soon had to return because of damage they suffered in a storm at sea. As they sailed back into Kealakekua Bay they were met by thousands of hostile Hawaiians. A minor skirmish escalated into a major battle which resulted in the death of Captain Cook. A monument placed in a park in Kealakekua Harbor marks the exact spot where he fell.

At the same time that Captain Cook was discovering the islands, a powerful young Hawaiian leader was rising to power. Originally from Kohala on the Big Island, he was the nephew of the king of that island—King Kalaniopuu. He was a natural warrior and after Kalamiopuu died he fought a nine year war against his cousin Kiwalao. At the end of the war Kiwalao was dead and Kamehameha was crowned the new king of the Big Island of Hawaii.

The location of the Hawaiian Islands was now public knowledge and traders from Europe and America started showing up in Hawaiian bays and coves trading for precious sandalwood. One of the commodities these traders brought to trade in the islands was gun powder. King Kamehameha was one of many kings who saw the military advantage of this black powder.

No ruler had ever ruled over all the Hawaiian Islands and with that goal in mind the new king of the Big Island sailed for Maui with an army of 16,000 men. Kamehameha and his substantial force all but ran over the small force at Lahaina. From there he turned his forces across the short distance of ocean to Molokai, taking the island in one bloody battle. He then sailed for Oahu where he encountered his greatest resistance. Landing at Waikiki, the defending tribe on Oahu fought hard, giving up their island inch by inch. They were pushed miles up into the mountains to the cliff where the Nuuanu Pali lookout is today. There they were driven off the cliff to their deaths. Soon after the King of Kauai, realizing the futility of trying to defend his island, surrendered without a fight acknowledging Kamehameha's sovereign power over his island. At that point the Great King Kamehameha was then crowned the first ruler of all the Hawaiian Islands. Soon after he moved his royal court from the Big Island to the more centralized Lahaina on the island of Maui where he ruled over the islands.

Known today as Kamehameha the Great, he died in 1819. It is said that his 24 years as ruler were the most peaceful years that these warring islands had ever known. His rule had taken the Hawaiian Islands from a group of warring tribes completely isolated from the world to a time of peace and trade in a world market. His death would ironically mark a time of another great change in Hawaii, a change in the religion and economic climate of the islands.

Kamehameha's son Liholiho became the next king, Kamehameha II. In the beginning years of his rule he was considered a weak leader.

He led a wild existence carousing and drinking. Later in his life he became sober, got serious and became a good ruler.

Wisely, before he died, Kamehameha I had appointed his favorite wife Kaahumanu to be Liholiho's "queen regent." During Liholiho's

early years, basically absent from his post, Kaanumanu assumed a strong leadership role on the throne. She abolished much of the old taboos against women and was considered the island's first feminist. She knew the old Hawaiian ways were doomed in this new age and encouraged change. Soon sacred holy places were being burned and idols knocked to the ground. The Hawaiian people were left hanging, spiritually dismasted. But a new religion was on its way to the islands via a boat from America.

The missionaries' contribution spread over a wide area. The first church was built in Lahaina on Maui in 1828. Built by the Reverend Richards, the Wainee Church still stands today. These missionaries clothed the Hawaiian women and discouraged them from visiting the sailors on the ships in the harbor. Their influence on the Hawaiians began the battle between the drunken sailors that frequented Lahaina and the missionaries who were attempting to change the ways of the natives.

It was these same missionaries who first translated the Hawaiian language into a phonetic written form. Before, history on the islands had been preserved in sacred chants of holy men (alii). These chants were passed down generation to generation from the time of the gods Wakea and Papa. The Hawaiians believed that all the alii on the island were descendants from these gods.

Kaahumamu continued her pursuit of social change and continued working with the missionaries. She helped write the first Hawaiian version of the Ten Commandments. She helped set up schools so Hawaiians could learn to read and write, giving them the tools to explore the world of western civilization.

Old Stone church on the Big Island of Hawaii. Photo courtesy of Rick Baker

Historical Hawaii

Liholiho and his wife later died of measles on a visit to London. Their deaths left Kamehameha III in power at the age of nine. He struggled as a ruler, growing up with a number of personal problems, including drinking. He started a scandal when he proposed marriage to his sister. The new religious leaders of his time were outraged. Kamehameha III was a victim, trapped between an old and a new world. According to Hawaiian tradition he should marry his sister because she was the highest ranked royal person in the islands. According to Christianity this relationship with his sister was incestuous. The problem was further complicated by the fact that the two were very much in love. The king tried to solve the problem by going on a permanent alcoholic binge while his sister married a local king on one of the other islands. The two continued to see each other secretly. When she died in childbirth, the king was devastated.

The death of Kamehameha III's sister and lover had an overall positive effect on him. Her death sobered him and from that time forward he ruled with an iron hand. He ended his autocratic rule by instituting a constitutional monarchy ending Hawaii's feudal society. He wrote the first Bill of Rights and instigated a change in how private land passed hands. Before that time, Hawaiians hadn't believed land could be owned by anyone. All the land was owned by the king and his chiefs. Kamehameha III divided up portions of the land to the commoners.

Kamehameha IV reigned only from 1854 to 1862. The last in the family line was Kamehameha V, who encouraged the importation of foreign contract labor to work in the sugar fields. Thus began Hawaii's multi-racial character. With his death the line of Kamehameha ended. William Lunalilo was elected king by popular vote but died soon after his election.

A legislative election brought King David Kalakaua to the throne in 1874. Known as the merry Monarch, the king promoted the development of the arts and sciences in Hawaii. He wrote the words to the national anthem, and brought back the hulu, the traditional dance which had been nearly stamped out by the missionaries.

Kalakaua was also the first king of any county to take a trip around the world. He granted Pearl Harbor to the U.S. for use as a naval base, and is known for building the present Iolani Palace on Oahu in 1882.

The last ruling monarch of Hawaii was Queen Liliuokalani, Kalakaua's sister, who ascended to the throne after the king's death in 1891. Thinking the U.S. had too much influence in the islands, she attempted to strengthen the monarchy. A sugar tariff in 1890 caused a decline in the profits of sugar and she refused to work with the farmers to find a solution. The businessmen on the island launched a campaign against her. A small war began between the American

One of the many varieties of Starfish.. Photo courtesy of Rick Baker

Historical Hawaii

planters and the queen's personal guard. The queen was soon overthrown and was imprisoned in Iolani Palace. As the years passed she took to song writing. One of her most famous was the song "Alohe Oe."

In 1898, the U.S. Government annexed Hawaii as an incorporated territory, a political status it would hold for the next 62 years. After the Spanish American War the U.S. Government began to see the military advantage of having a base on Oahu. Pearl Harbor was dredged in 1908 and opened three years later. So began the military component in Oahu.

Pearl Harbor was attacked by Japan on December 7, 1941. On that day 2,325 U.S. servicemen and 57 civilians were killed. The Japanese destroyed 188 planes and 18 major warships were sunk. The attack focused the Americans' attention on Hawaii as the point of the outbreak of World War II. Martial law was declared, and many suspicious Japanese-Americans were jailed, although very few ended up on the mainland. Later, young Japanese–Americans were allowed to join the service and most of them formed the 442nd Regimental Combat Team which served with distinction in the European Theater.

Tourism began to return to Hawaii after the war, but not in great numbers, until 1959—the year that statehood and the jet plane arrived in the Islands simultaneously. This began the economic tourist boom that would change the face of these tiny little islands in the middle of the vast Pacific Ocean.

Chinaman's Hat. Photo by William Waterfall, courtesy of Hawaii Visitors Bureau

Land of Volcanos

Kilauea erupting on Hawaii. Photo by Peter French, courtesy of Hawaii Visitors Bureau

Land of Volcanos

Deep beneath the crust of the earth in a zone of the earth's interior called the mantle, a corkscrew-like plume of upwelling molten rock rises to one spot on the underbelly of the ocean's crustal plate. Heating and deforming the hard oceanic crust above it, this "plume" of magma brings with it intense heat which melts, then cracks the very floor of the ocean, finally punching a hole right through the earth's crust. On the sea floor a small volcano is born with layers of molten rock forming under the monumental pressure of thousands of feet of sea water above. As the volcano grows it reaches for the surface of the sea and finally breaks the surface, forming a volcanic island in the middle of the largest ocean on earth — the Pacific.

This is how Kauai, the northernmost island in the Hawaiian chain, was geologically formed. That might have been the end of the story except for a little known fact concerning the sea floor, or more scientifically, the crustal plate of the Pacific ocean; the plate is moving. Floating on the molten mantle deep in the earth, the oceanic crust that makes up the floor of the ocean is being pushed northeastward by geologic forces. These forces find their origins at the East Pacific Rise, a long submarine mountain range thousands of miles to the south of the Hawaiian Islands. It is there at the crest of this mountain range that oceanic crust is originally formed, then pushed away to begin its journey northeastward. As the sea floor moves it takes the islands along for a ride. But the corkscrew plume of hot magma deep in the bowels of the Earth remains stationary.

After Kauai was born, the ocean floor continued on its northern trek. As the ocean floor moved northward the volcanic plumbing that had supplied the volcano on Kauai with molten rock was severed and a new hole was punched in the sea floor south of Kauai.

Haleakala Crater on Maui. Photo courtesy of Rick Baker

Again on the ocean floor a volcano was born which rose to the surface and became Oahu. Later, when it was again time for a new volcano, Maui, Molokai, Lanai and Kahoolawe were formed as one giant volcano which later subsided, allowing Pacific water to flood the crater which is now the watery space between these islands. On the Big Island of Hawaii, the volcano building process is still occurring. Of the five volcanos that make up the island, Kilauea and Mauna Loa are still active.

The Hawaiian Islands are the tops of an underwater mountain range that stretches north beyond Kauai some 1500 miles across the floor of the Pacific Ocean. There are eight main islands—Hawaii, Maui, Kahoolawe, Lanai, Molokai, Oahu, Kauai, and Niihau. These islands are just a few of the hundreds of volcanos that make up this mountain range, yet these high peaks in this chain account for 99 percent of all the above water landmass. This is because after a volcano is born and its umbilical cord is cut from mother earth, the force of erosion begins to take its toll.

As the new volcanos migrate northward, a natural erosional process cuts away at the island, adding volcanic sand to the beaches and producing lush soil for the rich vegetation that covers the Hawaiian landscape. Rivers rich in volcanic sediment and pounding waves against tall cliffs dump the very mountain itself back into the sea from which it came. Eventually the island is level with the sea. The once tall islands north of Kauai are today below sea level. Coral reefs, still growing upward toward the sunlight, are perched along their submerged flanks.

It is in this way that a Pacific volcano is born, grows to maturity, and then growing old, eventually

Following Page: Photo by Warren Bolster, courtesy of Hawaii Visitors Bureau.

Land of Volcanos

returns to the sea. This is always the way of nature. Even the mighty Pacific ocean plate must eventually return to the bowels of the earth. As it continues northward it collides with Alaska. Bending, the plate pushes under the continent forming a deep submarine trench. Deep in the bowels of the earth the ocean plate melts into magma which feeds the string of volcanos above called the Aleutian islands.

The story of the birth and death of volcanos is told piece by piece in the landscape of each of the Hawaiian Islands. On the Big Island of Hawaii the story of birth is told in a very dramatic way. This is the youngest and the largest of all the islands. Kilauea, Hawaii's most active volcano, has recently added almost 100 acres to the Big Island's total real estate. The continual eruption of Kilauea and Moana indicates the island is still growing and still over the hot spot.

Mauna Loa, the island's tallest peak, now rises above sea level to a height of 13,677 feet. This makes Mauna Loa one of the tallest mountains on earth at a overall height of 31,677 feet above the sea floor.

From Maui to the north, the gradually sloping profile of Mauna Loa is very noticeable. It almost resembles a giant shield lying face down on the floor of the Pacific. For this reason, geologists call Mauna Loa and all the other oceanic volcanos around the world shield volcanos. Volcanos on the continent, like Mount St. Helens, have very steep slopes. As you move north along the Hawaiian Islands, one by one to older and older volcanos, this shield-like profile becomes harder and harder to see. The forces of erosion can completely change the face of a volcano.

Not worried about erosion at this time, Kilauea is the newest member of the volcanic clan on Hawaii and is only 4,093 feet above sea level. It has been active since 1983 giving the northern side of the island a new face lift on a regular basis.

The Hawaiian fire goddess, Pele, is said to live in whichever volcano is presently active. As walls of hot lava approached Hawaiian villages, legends tell of the holy men who placed themselves and sacred branches in the path of the lava to appease the fire goddess and save the settlement from certain doom.

As you would expect, this fire goddess is easily put off. For instance, legend has it that if a visitor takes home a piece of lava they will later experience bad luck. Returning the rock to the island, even by

View of the Big Island from Haleakala Crater on Maui. Photo courtesy of Rick Baker

Land of Volcanos

mail, will break the spell. There is a case in the visitor center with a display of rocks returned with notes of apology mournfully attached.

Not all molten lavas are the same. Continental volcanos have very explosive volcanic eruptions like the one that occurred on Mount St. Helens. This magma comes from re-melted oceanic crust which is lower in temperature and has a lot more gas and water vapor in it. These chemical conditions give the magma a higher viscosity. In comparison, magma from *Kilauea* or any mid-ocean volcano comes from deep in the mantle and is low in viscosity. That is why it flows like a river down the mountain top instead of exploding.

Hawaiian lava is very high in temperature as molten rocks go. They are actually the hottest magmas on earth. There are two types of lava on Hawaii. One is the high temperature pahoehoe lava which flows swiftly down the mountaintop like a river. As it cools, gasses escape and the molten rock becomes thicker, more slow-moving and crumbly. This lava is called a'a by the Hawaiians.

Swift moving rivers of molten rock racing down the flanks of the volcano cool down in an interesting way, forming very distinct geologic formations called lava tubes. This happens when pahoehoe is confined to a channel on its way down to the sea. As the flow begins to cool the edges and top cool first. This solidifies and becomes an insulating cap rock that allows the lava beneath it to run freely on its way to the sea. If the volcanic eruption dies out at the top of the volcano or if the lava gets re-routed down another tube, the remaining lava flows out into the sea leaving behind what is called a lava tube. Many of these tubes are accessible from the sea and make for some pretty exciting diving.

Haleakala on Maui was the last volcano to erupt there. Much erosion has hidden the volcanic nature of this island, yet on the top of Haleakala which last erupted in 1790, you'll find a spectacular volcanic terrain. The mountain is 10,023 feet tall and as you drive up to the crater's rim, the landscape begins to transform from a lush green jungle to a very stark, barren land. At the top cinder cones, ash and pumus dominate the land which looks very much like a lunar landscape.

The next oldest volcanic island is Oahu. Near Waikiki Beach, Diamond Head looms in the background. Diamond Head is officially called by geologists a "tuff cone." Tuff cones are formed when lava is injected into the sea. Underwater, this lava cools very quickly and in such a way that it crystalizes out into tiny ash fragments. As these fragments pile up they consolidate forming a cone shaped formation called a tuff. At the site of the National Memorial Cemetery at Punchbowl crater a similar geologic formation exists.

To the north, on Kauai, the volcanic origins of this island have almost been completely covered by nature's erosional forces. This volcano is highly eroded and it is for that very reason that it is the most beautiful of all the islands. The peak of the volcano is one of the

Diamond Head on Oahu as seen from Waikiki Beach. Photo courtesy of Rick Baker

Land of Volcanos

wettest places on earth with an annual rainfall of over 450 inches a year. Rivers flow down the volcano's peaks cutting deep canyons into the volcanic rock. Waimea Canyon is one of the biggest of these canyons. This red gorge is called by locals the "Grand Canyon of the Pacific." On Kauai's north coast the famed Na Pali coastline is another monument to

erosion. Rainfall and the unrelenting surf have cut deep V-shaped valleys, pointed ridges and vertical precipitous cliffs some 2,000 feet high. At the water's edge, sea caves, natural arches and spouting blow holes abound. Evidence of the original volcanic shield that was once such a noticeable feature of this island is gone, camouflaged by years of erosion.

To the north, the next volcano lies beneath the surface of the sea. A constant reminder to the once volcanic Kauai that volcanos are born, grow and eventually find their way back to the sea. In this way the Hawaiian Islands are collectively a collage depicting the life and times of an oceanic volcano.

Deep canyons cut through the interior of Kauai — a testament to the power of erosion. Photo courtesy of Ronald Owen

Climate & Language

Tropical Climate

The term "weather" really doesn't apply on the islands. The climate changes so little from summer to winter that it is hard to tell the seasons apart. Temperatures throughout the islands average about 80 degrees in the summer and 78 degrees in the winter. At night the temperature drops about 10 degrees. This, of course, doesn't apply to the mountain peaks where temperatures can drop as low as 40 to 50 degrees.

To divers, the weather is important because it can affect dive conditions on various shorelines around the islands. About 300 days of the year the trade winds blow from the north. This produces the world class wave heights that surfers love along the northern shores of all the islands. This is why for the most part there is very little diving in these areas.

You'll find that rain plays a small role in the dive conditions as it rains quite a bit on all the islands. Again, it is the wind that will be the deciding factor as to which spots you can or can't dive. It is best to contact your local dive store for more information.

The moderate temperatures on the islands can be attributed to the ever blowing trade winds. Their oceanic breezes blow about 300 days of the year from the northeast. It is because they blow with such regularity that the northeast

Skill and agility is needed for this windy climb. Photo courtesy of David McCray

Majesty displayed. Photo courtesy of Cory Gray

side of all the islands is called the windward side. The trade winds actually have a real positive side to them. They act as a natural air conditioner. For a tropical island, Hawaii is quite mild and the trades are responsible for keeping the islands both cool and dry. As the sun sets, these cool breezes die out. Given the near proximity of the islands to the equator, the humidity should be stifling. Yet, Hawaiians enjoy about a 50 percent atmospheric humidity. When the trades die down for a number of days, usually in the winter, the humidity skyrockets.

Not as common are the Kona Winds. These blow in the opposite direction, from the southwest. Usually warm and moist, these equatorial winds often bring bad weather or at least hot muggy air. They are most commonly experi-

enced between October and April. When these winds blow at this time of year they are hot. In the winter they are survivable. If you catch one in the summer, run for an air conditioned room. Storms that come out of the south, usually in winter, are strong and can be devastating.

You'll find that rarely a day goes by that it isn't raining somewhere on any one of the islands. On the windward side, where the trades blow, you can see evidence of all this rain with the lush jungles and streams filled with water. The leeward side of all the islands is quite arid, desert-like. It is only when the Kona Winds bring in a storm that the leeward side gets a good drenching and then it can be upwards of 3 inches an hour. Just a few miles in from the beach, on the windward side, rainfall can average 250 inches a year. On Kauai's

Mount Waialeale, average rainfall is in excess of 450 inches a year. Except when the Kona Winds are blowing, the best diving beaches are on the leeward side of the islands. Waves are small and these shorelines usually average about 15 inches a year. When it is raining you can usually move down the coast a short distance and get out of it or hang out and enjoy the warm rain.

The "high season" is the term used for the tourist season which extends from about two weeks before Christmas until Easter. June, July and August are also busy times for the tourist. Prices for hotels, car rentals and air transportation can be twice as high and completely booked. To avoid the crowds and get the best value for your dollar, avoid these times of the year.

Local Language

Until the missionaries began to write down Hawaiian words in the 1820s, the language was only spoken. They spelled each word phonetically using only 12 letters. Starting with seven consonants h,k,l,m,n,p,w, the missionaries then added the five vowels, a,e,i,o,u. The Hawaiian language has been influenced by the many cultures that call the islands their home, including English, Japanese, Chinese and Portuguese.

Another language used on the island is called Pidgin, (a slang language formed by the plantation owners to communicate with laborers that had just arrived from China, Japan or Portugal). A general knowledge of the language will help you get a feel for the culture, as well as help you get around the island as all the towns and street signs have Hawaiian names. Here are a few Hawaiian words you may find helpful.

Basic Hawaiian Language

a'a - type of lava
ae - yes
akamai - clever
ali'i - chief
aloha - hello or good bye
aole - no
hale - house or building
hana - work
haole - foreigner, or white person
hapai - pregnant
hapa - half
haupia - coconut milk pudding
heiau - temple
holomu - long dress
hoolaulea - festive event
hulu - angry
hui - society
hula - dress
huli huli - barbecue
imu - underground oven
ipo - lover
kalua - pork roasted underground
kamaaina - native of Hawaii
kane - man

kapu - forbidden
kaukau - food
keiki - child
kokua - help
kona wind - wind from the south
kapuna - grandparent, old timer
lanai - porch
laulau - steamed pork
lei - string of flowers
limu - seaweed
lomilomi - salted salmon
lua - bathroom
luau - Hawaiian feast
mahalo - thank you
mahimahi - dolphin fish
makai - toward the sea
malihini - a newcomer
manauahi - free
manapua - Maui potato chips
manini - cheap
mauka - toward the mountains
mauna - mountain
mauna - the ocean
muumuu - a dress

ohana - a family
okolehau - Hawaiian booze
ono - delicious
opu - belly
opihi - limpet
pahoehoe - type of lava
pakalolo - marijuana
pali - cliff
paniolo - cowboy
pau - quitting time
pilau - stink
pilikia - trouble
poi - a paste made from taro root
pono - excellent
puka - a hole
punee - bed
pupu - hors d'oeuvre
pupule - crazy
tapa - paper cloth
tutu - grandmother
ukulele - stringed instrument
wahine - young woman
wai - fresh water
wela - hot
wiki - fast

PART II
Traveling
The Islands

Getting There

Over five million tourists a year fly to the Hawaiian Islands to vacation. A central point in the expansive ocean, these islands also are a stop-off point for flights continuing on to other ports on the Pacific rim. For these and other reasons, this part of the world is one of the easiest to get to, and the jet is about the most common way to get there. About 10 major domestic airlines cross the Pacific and land on the islands. Prices can be extremely competitive. Package deals including airfare, hotel and car can prove to be some of the most competitive prices in the world.

The flight from the West Coast takes about five hours. When you arrive in Hawaii you will have gained 2 – 3 hours over Pacific Time. Flights are cheaper during the week if you can travel then. You are allowed two free pieces of luggage and a carry-on bag. The two main pieces can't weigh more than 70 pounds each. If you don't bring weights, you will find your dive bag well under the limit. I always feel better carrying my camera gear on the plane and storing it above my seat. Cameras are not counted as carry on. Make sure you put your name on everything. Any additional weight or bulky package will cost you a few dollars more.

At the turn of the century, an American law was passed that stipulated only an American carrier can transport you to and from two American cities. This law still applies today. To fly exclusively to Hololulu and back you must use an American carrier. If you plan to continue on to Japan stopping over in Hawaii, you can fly a foreign carrier. If a foreign port is your final destination and you want to fly a foreign carrier, contact a travel agent. Otherwise here is a list of the domestic carriers you can take to the islands.

Domestic Carriers

United Airlines
(800) 241-6522
Direct flights from San Francisco, Los Angeles, San Diego, Seattle, Portland, Chicago, New York, Denver, Toronto to Honolulu on Oahu. Also direct flights to Maui from San Francisco, Chicago, Portland and Los Angeles. From San Francisco and Los Angeles they fly direct to Kauai, as well as to Kona on the Big Island. A direct flight from Los Angeles to Hilo is also available.

American Airlines
(800) 252-0421
To Honolulu from Los Angeles, San Francisco, Dallas and Chicago. Maui is serviced by a direct flight from Los Angeles.

Northwest Orient
(800) 225-2525
Flights connecting in Portland, Oregon fly to Honolulu and then on to Tokyo, Osaka, Okinawa, Manila, Hongkong, Taipei, and Seoul.

Continental
(800) 525-0280
To Honolulu from Los Angeles, Houston, and Chicago.

Delta Airlines
(800) 221-1212
Los Angeles, San Francisco, San Diego, Anchorage, and Vancouver to Honolulu.

Hawaiian Air
(800) 367-5320
From Los Angeles, San Francisco, Portland, Seattle, and Anchorage to Honolulu.

Tour Companies

Tour companies offer packages which include air, hotel and car rental at prices that are very competitive. You don't even have to shop around much to get a great deal. For example, you can fly from the West Coast and spend a week in Hawaii (air, car, hotel) for a grand total of about $400 dollars. Some tours include hiking, camping or kayaking tours.

SunTrips
2350 Paragon Dr.
San Jose, CA 95131
(800) 786-8747

Island Holiday Tours
440 Mission Court, #245
Fremont, CA 94539
(800) 448-6877

Student Travel Network
7202 Melrose Avenue
Los Angeles, CA 90046
(213) 934-8722

Pleasant Hawaiian Holidays
2404 Townsgate Road
Westlake Village, CA 91361
(800) 242-9244

Hawaiian Holidays
440 Mission Court, #245
Fremont, CA 94539
(800) 367-5040

Bicycle Tours

Island Bicycle Adventures
569 Kapahulu Ave
Honolulu, HI 96815
(808) 732-7227

Backroads Bicycle Touring
1516 Fifth Street
Berkeley, CA 94710-1740
(800) 245-3874

Traveling the Islands

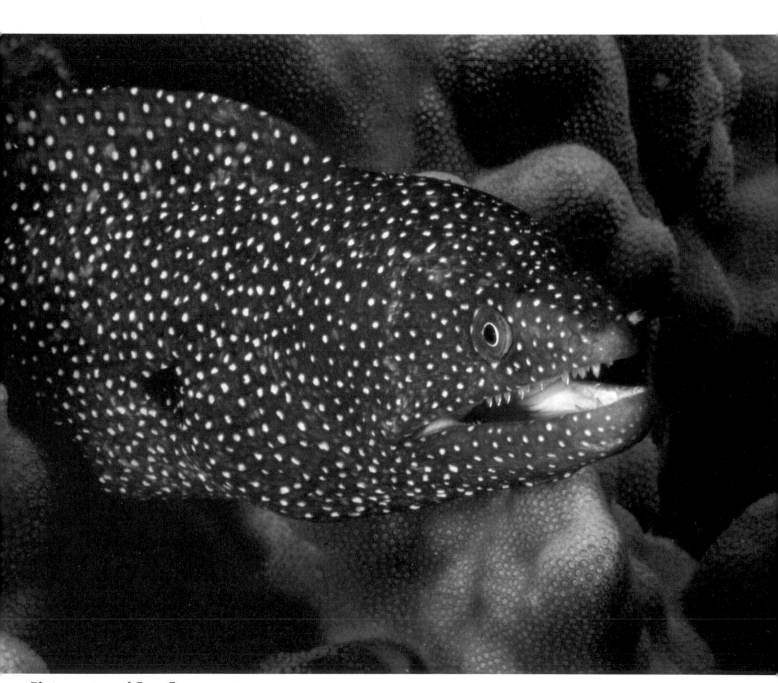

Photo courtesy of Cory Gray

Getting Around

One of the bizarre aspects of inter-island travel in Hawaii is that there is no way to get from island to island by boat. A few ferry services do exist and are mentioned in the individual chapters, but for the most part if you want to get from one island to the next you must fly.

The jet service is remarkably convenient. Flights run almost around the clock to any of the islands. Fares vary from about $50.00 to $70.00 dollars. Most flights are scheduled between 6 a.m. and 8 p.m. and take off every 20 minutes or so. Aircraft range from DC-9 or Boeing 737 jets to smaller turbo-prop aircraft for shorter runs. Flights vary between 20 and 40 minutes in length.

Hawaiian Airlines
(800) 367-5320 Mainland
Oahu - 537-5100
Maui - 244-9111
Kauai - 245-3671
Hawaii - 935-0811
Molokai - 553-5321
Lanai - 565-6429

Aloha Airlines
(800) 367-5250 Mainland
Oahu - 836-1111
Maui - 244-9071
Hawaii - 935-5771
Kauai - 245-3691

Car Rentals

At any Hawaiian airport you'll walk off the plane and run into dozens of car rental booths. The car is the best way to get around on the islands. You will see all the familiar booths like Avis, Hertz, National and Budget. Some of these rental agencies have some pretty stiff requirements, so before you leave home make sure you pass all of them. You must be 21 years old (some say 25) and possess a valid driver's license and you must have a major credit card. Some will take a deposit, but this can be quite

Wide variety of camping and hiking areas on all the islands. Haleakala Crater on Maui offers up some moon–scape terrain to explore. Photo courtesy Rick Baker

high. Again, if you have any doubt, check with the rental company before you get on the plane for Hawaii.

This is a very competitive market and you can get mileage-free deals for less than 10-15 dollars a day, especially if it is part of a package. Of course, you pay for the gas. There are a number of different types of deals and arrangements. It pays to shop around a little. Here are a couple of rental agencies:

National Car Rental
(800) 328-4567 Mainland
(800) 328-6321 Hawaii

Hertz
(800) 654-3131

Dollar
(800) 421-6868

Avis
(800) 331-1212 Mainland
(800) 645-6393 Hawaii

Budget (Sears)
(800) 527-7000

Camping & Hiking

In this book, in each of the island's respective chapters, you will find a full listing of all the parks and campgrounds. Parks are either national, state or county. The parks are well developed with thousands of hiking trails, campsites and incredible mountaintop views. These islands are actually little mini-continents where you can hike up a volcano through a dense jungle and step into a cold, barren volcanic crater and then continue down into an arid desert-like wilderness.

Hawaii has two national parks: one on Maui at the top of Mount Haleakala (Haleakala National Park) and Hawaii Volcanoes National Park on the Big Island of Hawaii. There is free camping and a permit required only if you want to use one of the cabins inside the crater on Maui.

Managed by the Department of Land and National Resources, Hawaii's 67 state parks include historic sites. Others allow limited camping. Each park is different so call or ask the ranger for information. Along the coastline of all the islands are the "beach parks" or county run parks. There are over 100 of theses parks and they range from a beautiful place to have a picnic to a full service campground. Of these, 36 have overnight camping. They do charge a few dollars a night to camp.

School of fish on the Hilton wreck off Waikiki Beach. Photo courtesy of Cory Gray

PART III
Diving Hawaii

Close—up of turtle off the Kona Coast. Photo courtesy of Cory Gray

The Dragon eel is one of many varieties of eel found in Hawaii. Photo courtesy of Cory Gray

Diving Hawaii

Water temperatures in Hawaii vary between 80 degrees in the summer to 72 degrees in the winter. Even if the water is 80 degrees at the surface it can cool down as you drop toward the bottom. An eighth-inch wetsuit, shortie or full length is recommended. Remember, water pulls heat from your body much faster than air (even 80 degree water). These suits also protect you from scratches you might get on the reef.

Great visibility is not a given in Hawaiian waters. When it is good it can exceed 100 feet. This usually occurs on calm days when the winds are not blowing.

When the winds are blowing, the warm gusts off the Pacific can make or break your dive. The trades blow everyday for the most part intensifying the surf on the northeast side of the islands (called the windward side). Less predictable are the Kona Winds which blow from the southwest (see Climate). When the Kona Winds blow, high surf plagues the leeward side (implies protected) of the islands. It is at these times that the windward side shows a friendly face to scuba divers.

There are those times when no winds blow and all parts of the island are accessible to divers. These times are rare and open up many relatively untouched dive spots.

One of the underwater features that makes Hawaiian diving unique is the lava tube. Lava tubes are hollowed-out, long caves where molten rock once flowed into the sea. These formations produce caves, caverns, ledges and drop-offs that create a spectacular underwater terrain for divers to explore.

You will find a wide variety of sea life within these cracks and crevices formed by volcanic lava

Humuhumunukunukuapau'a is Hawaii's State fish. Photo by Marjorie L. Awai, courtesy of Hawaii Visitors Bureau

flows and around the coral reefs that grow on them. Fish are plentiful with small, white damselfish or the colorful striped moorish idols darting about the reef. The butterfly fish, resembling the wings of a butterfly, punctuates this strikingly beautiful underwater terrain. Along the reefs you will also find parrotfish, wrasses, surgeonfish, tangs, trumpetfish and forcepsfish.

The range of possible underwater encounters is overwhelming. Jump into the water and experience a moray eel or a shark on the reef, surprise a school of spinner dolphins, a green sea turtle or a manta or eagle ray. Or if you're one of the lucky ones you might go eye-to-eye with a humpback whale. If you don't actually see these magnificent creatures, you may hear them as they sing their love song to the sea.

Hawaiian Whales

Like all mammals, whales are warmblooded, give live birth and nurse their young. They must breathe air to survive but can usually stay underwater for 20 minutes to an hour. The scientific name for a whale is cetacean. The order of Cetacea includes porpoises, dolphins, toothed and baleen whales.

Dolphins and porpoises are toothed whales and eat fish and squid, chewing very little with their teeth. Their stomachs actually do most of the grinding. In contrast, baleen whales have a giant, fine strainer that is attached to their gums. With this strainer they filter ocean water, removing plankton and tiny planktonic crustacean called krill.

Whales use a combination of a unique internal sound system and their hearing to navigate and communicate. Sending out a clicking noise, the sound bounces off the surrounding underwater terrain, helping them to navigate. Some of these sounds can be heard across the ocean for many miles.

One of the big mysteries about whales revolves around their intelligence. Whales have a brain size to body weight ratio comparable to humans. The cerebral cortex, where higher brain functions occur, is very well developed in whales. How these animals express this higher order of intelligence is unknown.

Humpback whales bear their young in the channel between Maui, Molokai and Lanai. The best time to see them is in the months of November through May. In the summer they migrate to the polar

Coral head off the coast of Oahu. Photo courtesy of Rick Baker

regions off Alaska's shores to feed on the large supply of plankton and krill in the water there.

Humpbacks live in groups called pods. Newborn calves are born underwater and pushed to the surface by their mothers so they can take their first breath. A baby humpback is about 16 feet long and weighs about 3,000 pounds. Adults average 50 feet in length and weigh about 50,000 pounds. Their average life span is about 30 years.

Humpback whales make a singing sound which has produced a lot of speculation among experts over the years. The "songs" are decipherable, vary from whale to whale and

Green Sea Turtle swimming off the Kona Coast. Photo courtesy of Cory Gray

are repeated over and over again. Some of these songs last for 20 to 30 minutes and can repeat for hours.

Humpbacks are an endangered species. At one time 35,000 humpbacks roamed the sea; today there are only a few thousand left. It was because whales originally picked the shoreline of Maui as their summer home that whaling villages like Lahaina sprung to existence in

the 1800's. No part of the whale went to waste. Today we have synthetic substitutions for every part of the whale at competitive prices. We must discontinue the slaughter of these fellow citizens of our planet earth.

Hawaiian Invertebrates

Some of the marine life on coral reefs in the Hawaiian Islands are found no where else in the world. But for the most part, the warm water distribution of reef organisms runs throughout the Pacific Ocean and, for that matter, around the world. You may notice differences in species from one warm water spot to another, but generally these critters will seem familiar.

There are about one million identified invertebrate species and probably several times that number awaiting discovery. On coral reefs most organisms which are not fish are invertebrates, though many invertebrates are mistaken by divers for plants or rocks. Some

invertebrates move around and are obviously animals. Others are attached to the reef, so plants cannot be distinguished from animals simply by their mobility or lack thereof.

Sponges

(Phylum *Porifera*)

Sponges are permanently attached animals belonging to the Phylum *Porifera*, meaning "hole-bearing." Some common sponges are large and conspicuous such as the Vase Sponge or the Venus Flowerbasket. Other less visible, but even more abundant, are the boring sponges, various species of the genus *Cliona*. They live in cracks and holes in the coral. Boring sponges dissolve the calcium carbonate skeleton of corals, eventually eroding coral heads from the inside and causing them to crumble. Sponges are filter feeders, pumping seawater through tiny pores all over their outsides. The water travels through internal canals to microscopic chambers where oxygen, and fine particles of food, are removed and carbon dioxide and metabolic wastes such as ammonia are dumped. The water is then pumped back outside. In large sponges, the water exits from the central cavity. If you dribble a few sand grains into that cavity, you will often see them suspended by the current of waste water. In small sponges, the water exits from a number of smaller holes. Sponges are extraordinarily efficient filters, removing particles below 1/25,000 inch in size. They can pump very large volumes of water. For example, an average size sponge can filter 400 gallons of water in 24 hours!

Sponges are reinforced internally by protein fibers and spicules, usually made of crystallized silicon compounds. Therein lies the rub. Have you ever patted a

Silhouette of diver hovering over a patch of black coral. Photo courtesy of David Mc Cray

fuzzy-looking cactus, only to discover some spines too small to see individually? Many species of sponges have microscopic spicules that can easily penetrate your skin or stick in your wetsuit and gloves. You will find them when you unsuit and touch bare skin. Also, some chemicals secreted by sponges are highly irritating to humans. Several species of sponges cause severe dermatitis.

Sponges are difficult even for experts to identify, and the safe ones can look a lot like the nasty ones. If you do touch sponges, don't even think of touching spicule-bearing gloves or hands to any important part of your body. If you get spicules in your skin they will cause mild to severe itching and dermatitis. Some people try to remove them with sticky tape, and scrap-

ing them off on a sharp edge seems to do as much or as little good. Others advocate rinsing with vinegar, mild ammonia, or meat tenderizer. Once in a while these remedies seem to reduce chemical irritation. You usually have to live with the spicules until they drop out after a couple of days, just as those little cactus spines do. In most cases, the problem clears up after a short while. Cortisone cream often helps. If the itching gets worse, see a doctor.

Hawaiian waters have many kinds of sponges ranging from the simple encrusting families to the large branching varieties. At one time Pearl Harbor was covered by large colonies of *Porifera*. Kaneohe Bay also provided the sheltered, protected conditions that sponges thrive in. The large sponges are

usually found at depths that exceed 200 feet.

Anemones & Corals
(Phylum Cnidaria)

Anemones, corals, gorgonians, and jellyfish are all in the Phylum *Cnidafia*, the name derived from the Greek *cnidos*, or thread. All cnidafians have thread-like microscopic structures in their tissues. These structures include tangling, adhesive loops that snare prey, and hollow hypodermic tubes that pump stinging, toxic chemicals into animals that touch them. The stinging threads are called nematocysts, and are fired upon physical contact. Most nematocysts are harmless to humans, but there are a few exceptions such as those following. Cnidarians have soft, hollow, bodies with a centrally located mouth surrounded by tentacles. Most of the nematocysts are on the tentacles. Cnidarians are radically symmetrical, like the spokes of a wagon wheel. Whatever they capture with their nematocysts is inserted by the tentacles into the mouth. The prey is then digested inside the hollow body, and undigestible parts such as bones and shells are dumped back out at the mouth. Cnidarians also have nervous systems with sensors that respond to light, touch and taste. Some of them have pretty good eyes too.

Anemones

Anemones have bodies shaped like cylinders. They are usually stuck to the reef, but they can and do occasionally move about. Most anemones have nematocysts that cannot penetrate the thick skin of the palms of your hands or your fingertips. When you touch them, they feel sticky because they've fired their nematocysts into – but not through – this thick skin. The most conspicuous large Hawaiian anemone is the Radianthus papillosa which grows over a foot in length and grows over 300 tentacles.

Another common species is Anemonia mutabilas which is small (about 1 inch tall) and has over 300 tentacles. There is also the Nectothelia lilae which lives attached to a plant and can swim like a jellyfish when detached.

Sagartia pusilla is quite small with under 50 tentacles and can change color to match its environment. Sagartia longa is found in shallow water. It has short green and white tentacles, a soft body, and is light brown in color.

Corals

Corals are colonies of interconnected animals similar in structure to anemones. Individual coral animals have mouths and tentacles with nematocysts and feed as anemones do. Within colonies, the individual corals are genetically identical, since members of each

Tiger flatworm photographed off the Kona Coast. Photo courtesy of Cory Gray

colony occasionally divide in half or bud off to produce new members on the edges of the colony.

Partially encircling the islands of Kauai, Oahu, Maui, Molokai and Lanai are fringing reefs composed of these microscopic colonies of coral. Because the Big Island of Hawaii is relatively new geologically, there are no fringing reefs there. Near shore, newly formed sub-tidal reefs occur on the leeward side of the islands.

Corals are dependent upon microscopic internal plants called *zooxanthellae* or coraline algae. These supply organic compounds and oxygen to coral through photosynthesis which aids corals to crystallize calcium carbonate from which they make their hard skeletons. In return the coral produces needed carbon dioxide to the algae. This relationship between two species in nature is called symbiosis.

Reef building corals survive only in warm tropical waters where the temperature seldom goes lower than 68 or 70 degrees. Like the sea anemone, the polyp catches food with tentacles that it extends out into the water. An unwary passerby need only touch the tentacle to be paralyzed by hundreds of nematocysts and drawn into the mouth.

There are over 120 species and varieties of coral on Hawaiian reefs. Stony corals are the most common of the reef builders and are found in both shallow and deep water. Those that are in shallow, quiet water are generally more delicately formed, with slender, graceful branches. Those in deeper water adapt to their environment by being thick and flat. This also gives them more surface area to absorb the diminishing light at deeper depth.

In shallow, rough water you may find corals like the staghorn, elkhorn, lobe or cauliflower corals. Adapted for high energy, these corals grow quickly, regenerating from any damage caused by waves.

Gorgonians & Black Coral

Gorgonians include sea fans, sea rods and sea fingers. Their drying skeletons frequently stink up people's suitcases on the way to their mantles. They, too, are colonial cnidarians.

Gorgonians have flexible skeletons made of protein and calcium carbonate spicules. Some species have internal plants, as do corals. The more spicules, and the more closely fused to one another, the harder the skeleton. In other parts of the world, species with hard skeletons are harvested, sliced, polished and sold as jewelry. Red coral from the Mediterranean, for example, is a gorgonian skeleton. Sometimes gorgonians are passed off as black corals. Black corals are colonial cnidarians not closely related to gorgonians, but very similar in appearance.

Ranked among one of the most rare of corals, black coral survives best in water over 130 feet deep. It does survive in more shallow waters but usually in light-protected areas like a cave or beneath an overhang.

Jellyfish & Portuguese Men-Of-War

Jellyfish are cnidarians that swim through the water. Jellyfish have hollow bodies with a single, central mouth facing downward. Their nematocysts are borne on tentacles and mouthparts that hang down from the main part of the body. The body pulsates rhythmically to propel the jellyfish through the water in search of fish and plankton. There are about 200 species of jellyfish in the world. Most of them live in cooler waters, but there are many tropical species. Jellyfish are also called medusae, due to the similarities between their dangling, stinging, venomous tentacles, and the mythological monster named Medusa, who had poisonous snakes on her head instead of hair.

Despite their blobby appearance, jellyfish are more compli-

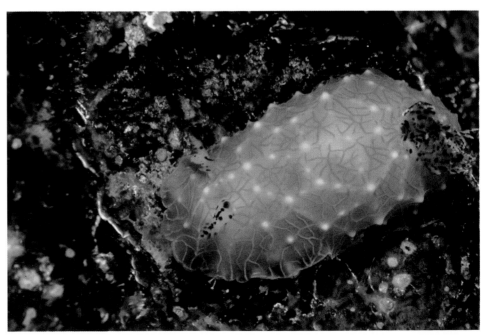

Nudibranchs are closely related to snails, but have no shells. Photo courtesy of Cory

Slate pencil urchin are common in Hawaiian waters. Photo courtesy of Cory Gray

cated than they look. At the base of their tentacles are light detectors and gravity receptors to keep them right-side-up.

There is a wide variety of jellyfish in Hawaiian waters. Two species are *Charybdea moseri* and *Solmaris insculpta*. *Charybdea* is a bell-shaped jellyfish that can be up to a foot wide. It has four tentacles which can seriously injure a diver or snorkeler. Also look out for a bluish-green, flat-looking jellyfish two or three inches in length called *Velella pacifica*.

Another curious and dangerous jellyfish called sea wasps are more common in Australia but do exist in Hawaiian waters. Sea wasps are small, clear jellyfish which swim near the surface at night. They spend the day in very deep water and are of no danger to divers then.

Sea wasps have squarish, transparent bodies, are usually from two to six inches long, and trail one or more tentacles from each lower corner of the body. The nematocysts on those tentacles can cause severe reactions, including local tissue destruction, extreme pain and even respiratory difficulties. When diving at night, be aware of sea wasps, but do not be intimidated by them. Remember, thousands of dives are logged all over the Hawaiian Islands every night without anyone getting stung. Furthermore, a little knowledge can greatly reduce your chances of getting stung. Here are some techniques which can keep you sting-free.

First, ask local divers where and when sea wasps are most abundant. Even if you get the OK, don't

assume that there aren't sea wasps present. Look before you leap. Scan the surface carefully before jumping off a boat or pier. When you ascend, look up before you come up. Sea wasps are most often sighted in the upper six feet of water. It is a good idea to avoid snorkeling on the surface at night, and to stay well below the surface during your dive. Wear full wetsuits and gloves at night in Hawaii, and keep your eyes open. Sea wasps can swim as fast as 20 feet per minute and may be attracted to lights. If you spot one with your light and it swims toward you, point your light elsewhere and get moving.

Portuguese Man-Of-War

The Portuguese man-of-war is not a true jellyfish, being related more closely to fire corals and stinging hydroids. The man-of-war has a gas-filled sac that floats on the surface. The float is up to eight inches long, and has a little sail which causes the man-of-war to travel with the wind. There are even right and left-handed men-of-war; the angle of the sail causes some to move consistently about 45° to the right side of the direction of the wind, and others to the left. Every man-of-war has long, trailing tentacles hanging below it. These tentacles are covered with nematocysts that are capable of catching fish, and you know that anything that can stop a fish cold in its tracks can penetrate human skin. The floats will tip you off to the danger. If you see them, stay well clear; the tentacles can be many yards long.

How to treat Cnidarian stings.

Small stings such as those from fire coral usually just hurt for an hour or so and go away on their own. Some divers claim that meat tenderizer can detoxify the venom and reduce the pain. Some get relief from cortisone cream on mild stings, but severe stings may require a shot from the doctor. If you get stung by a jellyfish or man-of-war, bits of tentacle will probably stick to your skin. Some of the nematocysts in these tentacles will have already fired, while others are still waiting their turn. If possible, try to avoid firing the nematocysts adhering to your skin that haven't yet been triggered. If you can lift the tentacles off gently and carefully with gloves, you will minimize the damage. Do not try to rub the tentacles off with sand; you will fire everything that is left on and into your skin.

Some biologists claim that alcohol can prevent nematocysts from firing, and the Australians keep big barrels of the stuff on their beaches to pour over sea wasp victims. However, some recent evidence indicates that alcohol may cause unfired nematocysts to fire! If you get badly stung by any cnidarian, you may need medical assistance, especially if you are prone to allergic reactions. If you are subject to severe allergic reactions from venom such as insect stings, it might be wise to skip night diving in the tropics.

Segmented Worms
(Phylum *Annelida*)

Non-divers often roll their eyes when told of the beauty of marine worms. That's because they have not seen them, and would not recognize them if they had. The worms most divers see on Hawaiian coral reefs are feather duster worms or spaghetti worms. These animals have long, segmented bodies divided into sections like a train. They are much more complicated in structure than the cnidarians. The worms have longitudinal nerve cords, circulatory systems with blood, primitive kidneys, muscles and intestines. With a mouth at one end and an anus at the other, marine worms are unlike cnidarians which have but one opening to eat and excrete through.

Feather Dusters & Spaghetti Worms

Feather dusters, *Sabellastarte magnifica*, live in a soft, membranous tube. They never leave their tube. Their spectacular fluffy brown and white plumes grow up to four inches across. Their plumes are combined respiratory and feeding structures. The worms pump blood through their plumes which take up oxygen and release carbon dioxide, and catch plankton and tiny food particles from the water. If you startle feather dusters, they will pull back into their tubes faster than the eye can follow. The feather duster worm has light-sensitive eyes just below the plumes. The mere shadow of a diver's hand is enough to make them retract rapidly.

The spaghetti worm, *Lanice conchilaga*, known to Hawaiians as kaunaoa, is usually found on reefs or in tide pools. Usually its body is hidden in a crevice with only its tentacles showing.

Sea Stars & Sea Urchins
(Phylum *Echinodermata*)

The word "echinoderm" means spiny skin. The echinoderms include sea stars and sea urchins. Like cnidarians, echinoderms are radially symmetrical. Most of them have five similar sections radiating out from their centers, like the segments of an orange. Echinoderms have hard internal parts made primarily of calcium carbonate. In echinoderms such as sea cucumbers, these pieces are not connected to one another, allowing the animals a great deal of flexibility. In other groups such as urchins, the pieces are fused together for strength, forming a rigid sphere that sometimes is reincarnated in shell shops as a night light.

Perhaps the most striking anatomical feature of the echinoderms is their hydraulic system. Many of them, such as sea stars and urchins, have tiny tubular feet between their spines. These tube feet can be extended by changes in water pressure within them. The animal takes water in through a filtering screen and pumps it through internal channels to wherever it is needed for locomotion. The hydraulic system supplements the muscles. It is used by urchins to rotate their spines, by cucumbers to pull back into their holes, and by brittle stars to move their legs.

Sea Urchins

There are many kinds of sea urchins in Hawaiian waters. Urchins have a tarnished reputation because some can cause immense pain with their spines, but most cannot puncture human skin. For example, pencil urchins have thick, blunt spines frequently used for wind chimes and jewelry.

There are more than 700 species of urchins in the world but in Hawaiian waters only 20 types of urchins can be found. The urchins with long spines can be very painful if you bump against them on the reef. The barbed tip can penetrate the skin very easily. While the wound is not fatal to man, it is extremely unpleasant.

There is evidence that these urchins are essential to the health of coral reefs by grazing away microscopic organisms that would otherwise overgrow living corals. The long-spined sea urchin has good light sensors and can detect fish or divers swimming overhead. When it does this, it swings its spines into position, pointing directly at the possible threat.

Some people advocate urinating on the wound or soaking it in vinegar to dissolve the spine. Others suggest pounding the tissue around the spine to break it into tiny bits, while others just leave it alone. The spine or its crushed products will eventually dissolve in the body and/or fester and be rejected, but it takes a couple of weeks or more. Urchins are another good reason to have a current tetanus shot before you dive. If you are prone to allergic reactions, or if the wound is deep, you should visit a doctor. There is a mild toxin on the spines that seems to cause much of the local pain. Little can be done to disinfect urchin punctures, but Neosporin or other similar products may help.

Brittle Stars & Basket Stars

Brittle stars and basket stars are echinoderms that have long, skinny arms which catch particles drifting in the water. Brittle stars are often seen on the outside of sponges, looking like spiders. They take advantage of the feeding currents that the sponges produce. Basket stars have five arms also, but they are highly branched, making them look like a huge bird nest. They can capture small fish and shrimp, as well as plankton. If you touch them gently (do it only once, please!) when they are expanded, they feel sticky and will writhe and wriggle their arms. Lights will also make them contract into a ball.

Crinoids

Crinoids, or feather stars, are often seen but not always recognized by divers. The arms feel sticky because they are used to catch plankton. This class of echinoderm is plant-like in appearance and is considered among the most attractive of sea animals.

The Crown of Thorns Starfish can grow up to 2 feet across. Its back is covered with sharp spines which have a toxic substance on them. This critter moves about with hundreds of tube-like feet.

Crustaceans

On the basis of sheer numbers and diversity, the arthropods are the most successful group of animals ever to have evolved on earth. Most members of the phylum are insects, which are very poorly represented in the ocean. Nearly all of the arthropods which live in the ocean are crustaceans, a group with about 30,000 species. Crustaceans include groups such as barnacles, shrimps, crabs, and lobsters. The crustaceans have jointed legs (arthropod means "jointed foot"), a hard outer covering called an exoskeleton that is periodically shed, and complex nervous, digestive, circulatory, reproductive and excretory systems. They reproduce sexually, and many of them have internal fertilization followed by external broodings of eggs. Crabs and lobsters "in berry" are females carrying fertilized eggs on the outside of their body. Their eyes are excellent, as any diver who has tried to sneak up on a lobster during the day knows. Crustaceans are about as complicated in structure as invertebrates get. There are hundreds of species of crustaceans associated with coral reefs, but the largest and tastiest ones usually are of most interest to divers.

Crabs

Among the better known crabs is the Serrate Swimming Crab, known to Hawaiians as the "Samoan Crab." It is a large crab and good eating. One of the more popular crabs in Hawaii is the Red Frog Crab, better known as the Kona Crab. It burrows backwards into the sand. It, too, is very good to eat. You may also run across the Red Hermit Crab. It is a deep-water species (50 feet or more). Also at this depth is the Hawaiian Swimming Crab, which seems to prefer the outside of reefs. Hermit crabs are also very common in these waters.

Shrimp

The Banded Squilla, or Banded Mantis Shrimp, is often found in Hawaiian waters. Resembling the Praying Mantis insect, it likes to live in muddy areas. It is edible and can reach lengths close to 1 foot. Other shrimps found offshore are Candy Cane and Harlequin Shrimp.

Slipper Lobsters

Cousins to spiny lobsters, slipper lobsters look like a cross between a squashed bulldog and a lobster. There are a number of Hawaiian species of slipper lobsters. One of the most rare is the Regal Slipper Lobster. These lobsters have no claws or long antennae, and are flattened. They get up to a foot long, but most are smaller. Like the spiny lobsters, they hide during the day and feed at night. If you find something that's not quite a crab or a lobster, and is tan or brown, it's probably a slipper lobster.

Spiny Lobsters

Most Pacific lobsters lack the large front claws that distinguish them from the Atlantic variety. The Long-handed Spiny Lobster does have pincers even though they are very small. The Western Lobster is found in Hawaiian waters and is considered to be the only true lobster found there.

Spiny lobsters are probably the single most desirable food sought by divers. If you take lobsters, be sure you know the local game laws and the local politics with respect to commercial lobster fishermen. If lobsters are in season where you are diving, there is probably a minimum size limit on them and a maximum bag limit, and most likely a prohibition against taking females carrying eggs. Even if there isn't, it is bad sport to take small lobsters or females in berry. Many areas prescribe the gear that may be used to take lobsters, too. A number of areas do not permit taking of lobsters with scuba, or with any tools other than your hands.

Molluscs
(Phylum Mollusca)

Molluscs are complex organisms and share some features with the arthropods. They have circulatory systems with a heart, a nerve cord and good eyes, a gut with a mouth at one end and anus at the other, and a file-like structure in the gut called the radula that grinds the food. Some molluscs, such as squids and octopuses, have eyes that rival our own in their ability to resolve images. The octopuses in

particular have fine wiring; they can be trained, and their brains are capable of abstract problem solving and learning to recognize geometric shapes. Most of the molluscs in coral reefs are hidden from view. The majority of them are clams, tucked deep into holes they have bored in coral skeletons, or down in the sand. The few molluscs that are often seen are fortunately some of the most spectacular representatives of the phylum. Coral reefs are good places for divers to spot squid and octopus, and the sandflats near reefs are usually inhabited by conchs and other large snails. Molluscs are very popular with divers who collect shells. The essence of collecting is that collectors should, ideally, not be able to collect everything in their field of interest; there should always be that one additional item needed to complete the collection. Mother Nature has been kind to shell collectors; there are over 100,000 species of living molluscs known, and most of these have shells. Recently, this has worked to the detriment of some beautiful species. When shell collectors were limited to whatever washed up on beaches, their impact on marine life was minimal. However, since divers can easily get at many previously rare shells, some species have been driven nearly to extinction in a few decades. Even if local regulations permit you to take living shells, please consider bringing home a photograph instead, and leave the animal alive and well on the ocean bottom.

Chitons

Everyone who dives from shore will wonder sooner or later what those inch long oval depressions are next to the water, and what those little creatures that look like pill bugs in each depression might be. They

are chitons, creatures which have been on Earth for about 600 million years. They are among the most primitive of molluscs. Chitons have eight overlapping calcium carbonate plates on their backs, making them look a bit like pill bugs, and a fuzzy band around their outer edges. On the West Coast, plates from chitons were used as wampum by North American Indians. Those depressions are exactly the right size for their inhabitants because chitons customize the rock a bit at a time, leaving their spots at high tide to graze, and returning to nestle down into the same location. Over a period of years, they gradually enlarge their depressions. It is a mystery as to how each chiton finds its way back to its own depression after feeding. Some biologists have theorized that the bits of iron-containing minerals that chitons have in their radulas allow them to sense the earth's magnetic field. If this is true, a chiton's radula is an internal compass which directs the chiton home.

Marine Snails

Conchs are large snails that crawl slowly along in sandy areas, especially in seagrass beds. Their shells often grace gift shops and their muscular feet often grace restaurant platters.

Nudibranchs

Nudibranchs are closely related to snails, but have no shell. They carry their gills exposed on their backs hence the name "nudibranch," which means "naked gill." Despite their apparent vulnerability to predators due to the lack of any hard protection, nudibranchs are rarely bothered by other marine animals. The reason for this is that nudibranchs seem to be highly repulsive or poisonous to many animals that might otherwise eat them. In fact, a number of nudibranchs actually eat cnidarians, but somehow keep their nematocysts from firing during the digestive process. These unfired nematocysts are then transferred by the nudibranchs to their gills, where they provide additional protection. Cold water divers probably know that many nudibranchs are brightly colored. Biologists call this "warning coloration," which tells a predator he is dealing with a nasty "don't bite me" nudibranch. Common nudibranch in Hawaiian waters are the Spanish dancer and phyllidia nudibranch.

Squid

Most squid in Hawaii are quite small, generally less than a foot long, with a fat little body and ten short arms. They are commonly found swimming in groups of three or four, changing colors rapidly from white to green to brown. You have a better chance of getting a close-up photograph by skin-diving rather than using scuba. They seem to be spooked by bubbles. Don't bother to try to sneak up on them. Their eyes are probably just as good as yours. Just swim slowly along and edge near them. If you try to rush them, you may get close for a kick or two, but they will sometimes pump out a burst of ink and jet away.

Octopus

Octopuses are the undercover camouflage champions of the reef. They crawl along the bottom, changing their colors and patterns to match their surroundings. They can go from near black to white and back as fast as you can blink, and can reproduce the appearance of cobbles, sand and almost anything they are near. They are active predators, seeking out fish, lobsters, crabs, and other large prey at night, and hiding during the day. When they catch something with their eight sucker bearing arms, they can bite it with a beak that lies in the center of the arms on the underside.

There are two species of octopus in Hawaiian waters: the day octopus, Octopus cyanea, and the night octopus, Octopus ornatus. Of the two, the day variety is the most common and can be found in shallow water along the reef. It is gray or brown and has a black spot below its eye and can have arms close to two feet in length.

The "night" octopus is smaller and not as common as its daytime counterpart. It is reddish brown or orange in color with patterns of dashes on its arms. These octopus were considered valuable to ancient Hawaiians in curing sickness caused by sorcery.

References:
Diver's Almanac : Guide to the Bahamas & the Caribbean (Caribbean Invertebrates by George S. Lewbel)
Pacific Marine Life by Charles DeLuca, Diana Macintyre.

Following page: Lanai offers some very interesting cave and cavern diving. Photo courtesy of David McCray

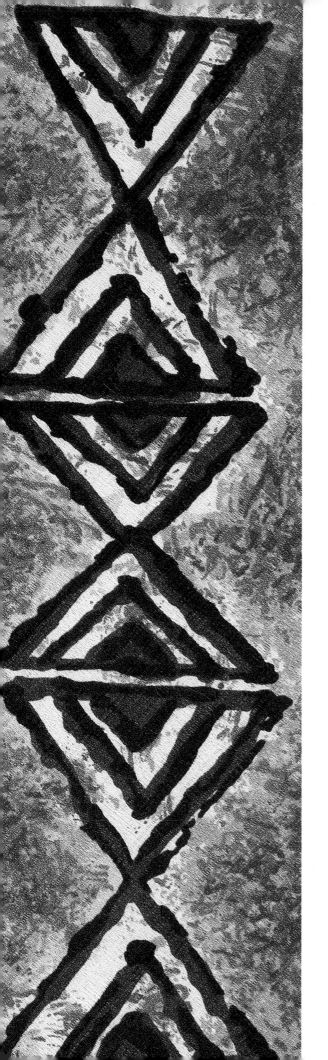

PART IV
The
Islands

PACIFIC OCEAN

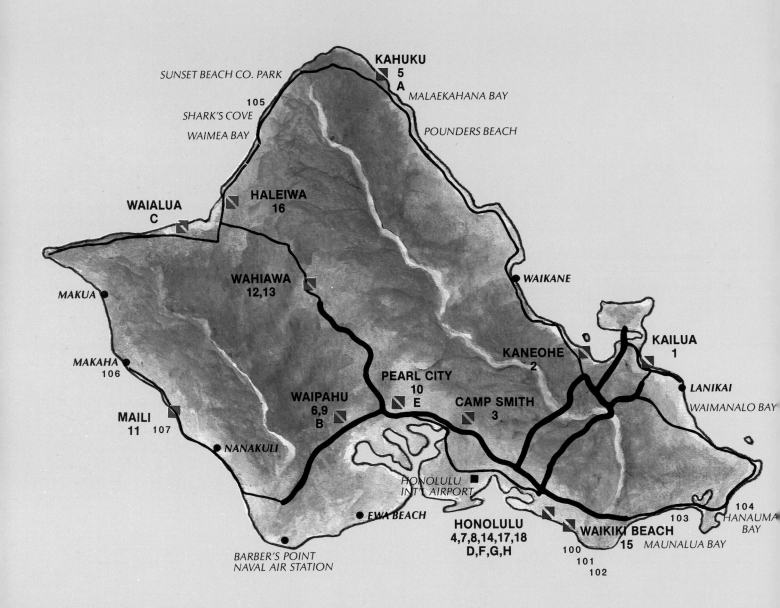

KAHUKU
5
A

SUNSET BEACH CO. PARK

MALAEKAHANA BAY

105

SHARK'S COVE

WAIMEA BAY

POUNDERS BEACH

WAIALUA
C

HALEIWA
16

WAHIAWA
12,13

WAIKANE

MAKUA

KAILUA
1

KANEOHE
2

MAKAHA
106

LANIKAI

WAIMANALO BAY

PEARL CITY
10
E

WAIPAHU
6,9
B

CAMP SMITH
3

MAILI
11 107

NANAKULI

HONOLULU
INT'L AIRPORT

EWA BEACH

104

HANAUMA
BAY

HONOLULU
4,7,8,14,17,18
D,F,G,H

WAIKIKI BEACH
15

103

MAUNALUA BAY

100
101
102

BARBER'S POINT
NAVAL AIR STATION

PACIFIC OCEAN

N

THIS MAP IS NOT TO BE USED
FOR NAVIGATIONAL PURPOSES

Oahu
The Gathering Place

Legend has it that in early Hawaiian times, the island of Oahu was the central governing island, a meeting place for all the outer island kings. These island kings came to Oahu to confer with the great King Kamehameha, the first to rule over all the Hawaiian Islands. The nickname "The Gathering Place" caught on and still applies today, as the state capital of the state of Hawaii is located here in Honolulu.

About 600 square miles, Oahu is the third largest island in the chain and hosts the largest population. Home to over one million people, Honolulu, the capital city of the state, has a population of over 900,000. The island hosts more than four million visitors a year. Many decide to stay and make this island their home.

There is a great diversity and number of activities on the island of Oahu. But, if you look a little deeper you'll find there is also another side to this island. There is an historical side that is reflected in the many museums and restored historical sites. The island boasts botanical gardens, aquariums and cultural classes, along with an exotic cosmopolitan atmosphere, hiking, camping and an excellent public transportation system. Or you could actually spend all your non-diving time hanging out on the beach. The choice is all yours.

Exploring Oahu
Waikiki Beach

There is something unique and classically Hawaiian about the surf at Waikiki Beach. For centuries gentle, slow, repetitive waves have caressed this famous shoreline. It is pure entertainment just to sit under a palm tree at one of the many beachside establishments, sip on a cold drink and watch the people on surfboards and in Hawaiian catamarans ride these waves in from hundred of yards offshore. Riding on waves was invented here, hundreds of years ago. Experiencing these waves firsthand lets you share a bit of Hawaiian history. The beach is lined with rental places that will be glad to set you up with a surfboard, lessons, canoe or catamaran ride, or just about any thing else you might need.

It was in 1901 that the first hotel was built here and in those days it was called the Moana Hotel. Today the newly restored hotel is a part of Hawaiian history and is called the Sheraton Moana Surf-

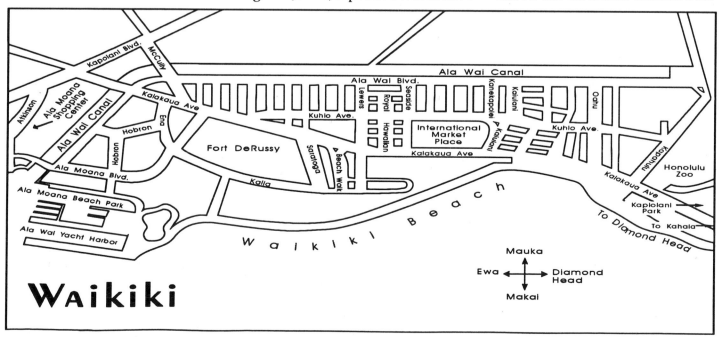

rider. A shady outdoor restaurant and bar opens out onto Waikiki beach. The hotel still reflects the old fashion charm of an earlier age and a time when thousands of people didn't compete for space on the beach.

Waikiki is currently a city of highrises, which include some 36,000 rooms in 125 hotel and condominium units. This is also the place for shopping. Within walking distance of most Waikiki hotels along Kalakaua or Kuhio Avenues there are numerous shopping centers. In this general area you'll find The **Royal Hawaiian Shopping Center** or the **Waikiki Shopping Plaza**. Make sure you take in the **International Market Place**.

Also within walking distance is the Kapiolani Park where you can take in the Kodak Hula Show, Waikiki Aquarium and Honolulu Zoo.

Driving Through Hawaiian History—Road Tips

To get around Honolulu and the rest of the island you will need something more than your feet. TheBus system here is excellent so don't be afraid to jump on TheBus and take a few short hops around Honolulu. The parking situation is so bad around town that TheBus might be less trouble than taking your car.

Sandwiched between the highrises and McDonalds hamburger stands are preserved historical sites and museums that are guaranteed to transport you back in time to the days of the early Hawaiians. For example, at the **Bishop Museum** in Honolulu you can get a measure of the greatest monarch ever to live on the island: King Kamehameha I. Born in 1758 on the Big Island of Hawaii, he rose to power defeating tribe after tribe until he was the first undisputed monarch of the Hawaiian Islands. His legacy

Windward Oahu commonly known as "The Pali." Photo courtesy of Cory Gray

began on the cliff above Pali, a short drive up the **Nuuanu Valley** (Hwy 61) where King Kamehameha's armies pushed the last defenders of Oahu over the cliff. On the way up Highway 61 to the Nuuanu Valley you will pass

Punchbowl, an almost perfectly round extinct volcanic crater where war veterans are buried from the Spanish American War to the Vietnam War. The road continues up to **Nuuanu Pali Lookout** where you can get a beautiful view of the windward Oahu. Below you will see the towns of Kailua and Kaneohe. Here at the lookout, it is easy to let your imagination go wild with images of warriors fighting with their last ounce of strength, then dropping off the edge of the cliff to their deaths. They still find bones at the bottom of the cliff. It was at this battle, this moment in Hawaiian history, that King Kamehameha became the first absolute ruler of all the Hawaiian Islands.

Continue on down the road to the bottom of the hill on the west side where the Pali Highway connects with two other roads. The first turnoff is to the left and takes you into Kaneohe where you can continue north up the windward northwest coast and on around the island (see Trip Around the Island). The second turn is to the right and will take you south around Diamond Head and back to Honolulu. This trip around Diamond Head takes around two to four hours depending on how many stops you make. The trip all the way around Oahu can be done in 4 hours, but if you plan to make some stops leave the whole day open.

Honolulu — Staying in Town

In Honolulu you can explore the **Iolani Palace**, the only royal palace in America. It was built in 1882 by King Kalakaua who was the last Hawaiian king with any real power before the Hawaiian Islands became a territory of the United States. He lived to see his powers as a king neutralized and himself become an inconsequential figurehead. These are guided tours only so make reservations.

When the **Aloha Tower** was built in 1926 its ten stories made it the highest building in the islands. Before planes brought people to these islands, ships pulled in here to load and unload passengers

Crowded Waikiki Beach. Photo courtesy of Rick Baker

Sunbathers on Waikiki Beach on Oahu. Photo courtesy of Rick Baker

from all over the world. Now the tower is used to observe ships coming in and out of the Honolulu Harbor. On the ninth floor of the tower you'll find the **Hawaiian Maritime Museum**. Piers 10 and 11 are usually the Saturday berths for inter-island cruise ships. At Pier 8 you can take the **Maui Princess**, a new passenger ferry boat to Molokai and Maui. Don't miss the *Hokulea*, the authentic re-creation of a doubled hulled sailing canoe that actually made the round-trip to Tahiti. Also in this general area is the *Falls of Clyde*, a 19th century square rigger.

At *Kewalo Basin* the fishing and diving charter boat fleet is moored. This is also where you can jump on a harbor cruise or catch a submarine ride.

The *USS Arizona Memorial* off interstate H–1 runs free tours every few hours from the visitor center. Boarding a launch, the tour takes you out to the memorial in the middle of the harbor. It was on December 7, 1941 that the Japanese attacked Pearl Harbor, sinking 6 ships and killing 3581 Americans, launching America into World War II. The Arizona sank in minutes with 1100 men on board. The tour takes a few hours and includes a presentation at the visitor center. Also here is the WWII submarine *U.S.S. Bowfin*. You can take a self-guided tour of the submarine. Open daily except Monday 8:00am to 3:00pm.

Trip Around the Island

To get out of town and around the island there are tour buses, vans or rental cars. There are two loops you can take to explore the island. One is to travel around the entire island which can take about four hours or a full day depending on how many stops you take. The other is up the Pali Highway to the windward coast, then turning south around Diamond Head returning to

Take a self-guided tour of the World War II submarine **USS Bowfin** *on Oahu. Photo courtesy of Rick Baker*

Waikiki Beach and Honolulu. This shorter version highlights some of the most beautiful beaches on the island.

You can circle the island in either direction but if you want to snorkel or dive at **Hanauna Bay**, it's best to get there early in the morning. Point your car down Kapahulu Avenue and turn on Diamond Head Road on the way to Diamond Head. This road will wind around and run into Highway 72 where you turn right. Continuing along Highway 72 you will come across **Koko Head**, not to be confused with Koko Crater nearby. Just a 15 minute hike reveals a beautiful view of Molokai across the channel and a interesting angle of Diamond Head and the Koolau mountains. As you continue you will so find **Hanauma Bay State Underwater Park**. Here an ancient, eroded, submerged crater from an extinct volcano provides some of the best snorkeling on the island. There are buses and tour vans that

will get you to this popular tourist spot if you just want to keep it simple and stay here for the day. Moving on down the road you will pass the **Halona Blowhole**. This is a lava tube positioned in such a way that it captures each wave, pressurizes it and fires it skyward for all to see — a spectacular sight. On down the road you'll find a very popular spot at the **Sea Life Park** where trained seals, whales, and dolphins will entertain you.

We have now entered the windward side of Oahu. Here the trade winds blow almost continuously and are always warm and balmy. Storms from the Pacific drop most of their rain here, producing the lush vegetation. As you approach Kailua you will encounter the Pali Highway (Hwy 61). You can take this over the mountains back to Honolulu or continue up Highway 83 to continue your trek around the island.

Near Kaneohe, at the Valley of the Temples Memorial Park, you will come across the road to a beautiful replica of a 900 year old temple called the **Byodo-In Temple**. The beautiful oriental garden setting also has a carp pool, massive nine foot Buddha statue and a teahouse. Continuing up the windward coast as you approach the town of Laie, you'll find the **Polynesian Cultural Center** which covers 42 acres and consists in part of 7 model villages representing island people from all over the Pacific.

When you reach Kahuku Point stay on Highway 83. You are now on the North Shore, famous for its world class surf conditions. Through the months of October

Facing page. Upper photo: The ornate butterfly fish looks like the Wing of a butterfly. Photo courtesy of Cory Gray

Lower photo: Hanauma Bay State Park. Photo courtesy of David McCray

through April, wave conditions and strong currents prevail. If it is summertime, go ahead and get wet! Some of the famous surf spots around here are beaches like **Sunset Beach**. Here you'll find the famous Banzai Pipeline which is unquestionably for expert surfers. Sunset Beach is two miles long but at times in the winter all the sand moves offshore leaving a reef and lava fingers. If you body surf or dive in the wrong surf conditions these "fingers" can be very hard on the human body.

As you approach Waimea Bay you'll see the sign for the **Puuomahuka Heiau**. Ignore signs warning that the road is too rough. The road is fine. The view of Waimea Bay from up this road is worth the ride. At the top you will find an authentic heiau where human sacrifice once took place. The stone work is spectacular. Just a short hop down Highway 83 you'll come to the road that will take you to the **Waimea Falls Park**. The drive up this small tropical valley that gets you to the park is beautiful and well worth the trip. This lush tropical valley leads to a botanical garden.

At the Kamehameha Highway turn south down through central Oahu. In the center of the island Oahu's two mountain ranges, Waianae and Koolau, rise on either side of the road ahead. This region is filled with sugarcane fields and pineapple groves. The Kamehameha Highway will soon turn into Route H2.

After a while you will run into Route H1. Turning left takes you back to Honolulu. Turn right to see the leeward side of the island. This is the only good road to the arid, and relatively untouched, leeward coast. You may want to take a tour or part of another day for this. This area is a last stand for ethnic Hawaiians, a place for locals. One place you can get a feel for the old

Diver playing with octopus off the coast of Kona on the Big Island. Photo courtesy of Cory Gray

Crown of Thorns Starfish can grow up to two feet across. Photo courtesy of Cory Gray

Oahu

days is at the **Plantation Village** and **Cultural Park** at Waipahu. Charter dive boats are anchored at Waianae harbor.

Getting There

Except for a few non-stop flights into Maui and the Big Island, most travelers to the Hawaiian Island pass through The **Honolulu International Airport**. There was a time when travel to the island was primarily by boat. Except for a few passenger ships, those day are long gone. Today almost everyone gets to the islands by plane. Honolulu is the busiest airport in the country with hundreds of flights daily from all over the world. These flights usually include a transfer to an inter-island carrier. Most flights from the U.S. are from San Francisco or Los Angeles and take about 4-1/2 hours. The inter-island terminal is separate from the main terminal and you need to take a shuttle between them. This can get to be a hassle if you're carrying a lot of gear and luggage. For more about the airport's layout and facilities see the section on Honolulu International Airport.

Airlines serving Oahu are *United Airlines, American Airlines, Northwest Airlines, Continental, Delta and Hawaiian Air*. Inter-island airlines include *Hawaiian Air* and *Aloha Airlines*.

Staying There

There are almost 40,000 rooms in over 100 hotels and condominiums in Waikiki. Prices are very reasonable on Oahu. Without even trying you can find a week long air-car-hotel package averaging about $500 dollars. You can stay in one of Waikiki's old restored historical hotels on the beach or in one of the high-rises a few blocks from the beach. The difference in price between a hotel room on the beach to one a few blocks inland might be quite substantial and worth investigating. Hotel rooms, condos and private homes are all available. In the condos you get a fully equipped kitchen for about the same price per night.

Most of the lodging on Oahu is found on Waikiki Beach, with a few exceptions. The island also offers state and county campgrounds where you can pitch a tent.

Honolulu International Airport

One of the busiest airports in the country, the Honolulu International Airport can become a source of frustration for the first-time traveler. Basically the problems come from the fact that there are two terminals. In the main terminal all the major international and mainland flights arrive and depart from Hawaii to points all over the world. The inter-island terminal is where

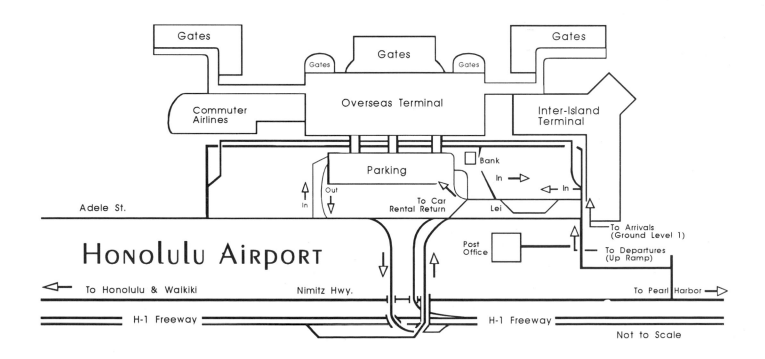

Oahu

the commuter airlines transport you to the outer islands. If you are carrying dive gear and luggage, getting from one terminal to another can become a hassle.

From the mainland you will first arrive at the main terminal. This two-story terminal is well equipped with lockers, long-term storage and car rental agencies on the first floor and on the second floor. For departing passengers there are ticket counters, lounges, shops and the entrance to most gates. From both the first and second floor you can board a taxi, TheBus or shuttle to your downtown hotel.

In the inter-island terminal you will find a snack bar, more car rental booths, lounges, information counter and restrooms. To get between the two terminals there are shuttles every few minutes. The walk takes about 5 to 10 minutes. Visitor Information: (808) 836-6413.

Camping & Hiking

Somehow, on Oahu, camping and hiking don't seem as socially acceptable as they do on the outer islands. Maybe it is the excitement of Honolulu and Waikiki Beach that kind of says "let's party" rather than "let's get away from it all." But as little as 10 minutes away from the city by car and another side of Oahu is revealed. There are some beautifully remote spots on this island.

Oahu has 23 state parks and recreation areas. Most are for day use only with hiking trails, showers and restrooms. Some have historical sites or are state monuments. Three of the state parks are open for tent camping: Sand Island State Park, near Honolulu, Keaiwa State Park, in the interior and Malaekahana State Park up the windward coast.

Of the 65 county parks, 13 are open for tent, trailer, and RV camping. You must get a permit and some parks may require a permit two weeks in advance. For information as to campground availability, contact the Department of Recreation.

To get away from the crowds, go hiking. Just a few minutes out

Lush vegetation lines the windward shore of Oahu. Photo courtesy of Cory Gray

of Honolulu and this island takes on a whole new dimension. One great hike is through dense jungle-like vegetation up by the historic **Nuuanu Pali**. To get there take the Pali Highway (Hwy 61) until you see the Old Pali Highway, turn right. Follow it to Reservoir No 2 spillway where the Judd Trail begins. This trail is a loop that will bring you back to your car.

One remote hiking trail will really get you back to nature and can be found up the windward side of the island at a site called **Sacred Falls**. You'll find a sign where you should turn off between Hauula and Punaluu off of Highway 83. To get to these falls you have to walk, but it's well worth the effort. There is a narrow part of the valley that leads to a slightly murky swimming hole. A great place for a picnic.

For more information about hiking contact:

Hawaiian Trail and Mountain Club
Box 2238
Honolulu, HI 96804

Hawaiian Audubon Society
Box 22832
Honolulu, HI 96822

Sierra Club
1212 University Ave.
Honolulu, HI 96826
(808) 946-8494

Parks
STATE PARKLANDS
Department of Parks and Recreation
650 S. King Street
Honolulu, HI 96813
(808) 523-4525

Division of State Parks, Oahu District
P.O. Box 621
1151 Punchbowl St.
Honolulu, Oahu, HI 96809
(808) 548-7455
Camping permits required.

Aina Moana State Recreational Area
East end of Ala Moana Beach Park near Waikiki Beach. High surf, snorkeling

Diamond Head State Monument
Off Diamond Head road. Hiking, nice view of Honolulu

Photo courtesy of Cory Gray

Hanauma Bay State Underwater Park
At Hanauma Bay Beach Park. Scuba diving, snorkeling, restrooms

Heeia State Park
Off Highway 836 at Kealohi Point. Pinicking, restrooms

Honolulu Stadium State Recreation Area
In Honolulu off South King Street. Picnicking, restrooms

Iolani Palace State Monument
In Honolulu at corner of South King and Richards. National historic landmark, guided tours
(808) 538-1471

Kaena Point State Park
End of Highway 930. Leeward shore and sandy beach

Kahana Valley State Park
Hiking, picnicking

Kaiaka State Recreation Area
North Shore, high surf at times. Snorkeling when calm, restrooms

Kakaako Waterfront State Recreation Area
At end of Ahui St in Honolulu (off Ala Moana Rd). Restrooms

Keaiwa Heiau State Recreation Area
End of Aiea Heights Dr. in Aiea. Camping

Malaekahana State Recreation Area
Off Highway 83, windward shore. Camping, snorkeling

Nuuanu Pali State Wayside
Off Pali Highway (Hwy 61). Scenic lookout

Puuo Mahuka Heiau State Monument
Off Highway 835. Oahu's largest Heiau - National Historic Landmark

Puu Ualakaa State Wayside
Nice view of Honolulu

Royal Mausoleum State Monument
At 2261 Nuuanu Ave. Burial place of Hawaiian royalty – guided tours

Sacred Falls State Park
Access by trail off Kamehameha Highway (Hwy 83)

Sand Island State Recreation Area
Off Nimitz Highway (Hwy 92) at end of Sand Island Rd. Camping, restrooms

Sans Souci State Recreation Area
Off Kalakaua Ave in Waikiki. Protected underwater marine park, snorkeling, scuba

Ulu Po Heiau State Monument
Off Kailua Rd (Hwy 61) in Kailua. Heiau ruins

Waahila Ridge State Recreation Area
In Honolulu at end of Ruth Pl. Hiking

Oahu

Wahiawa Freshwater State Recreation Area
At 380 Walker Ave off Highway 80

Waimanalo Bay State Recreation Area
About 20 miles north of Honolulu airport up the Pali Highway. Windward shore, swimming, restrooms

FEDERAL PARKLANDS

James C. Campbell
National Wildlife Refuge
c/o Hawaiian and Pacific Islands NWRs
P.O. Box 50167 or
300 Ala Moana Blvd.
(800) 541-1201

U.S.S. Arizona Memorial
No.1 Arizona Memorial Place
Honolulu, HI 96818
(808) 422-0561
Free tickets, boat tour of sunken battleship

COUNTY PARKLANDS

Honolulu City & County Dept. of Parks and Recreation
650 S. King St.
Honolulu, HI 96813
(808) 523-4525
Camping permit required

Ala Moana Beach Park
In Honolulu, off Ala Moana around Kamakee Street. Swimming, restrooms, showers

Aukai Beach Park
Off Kamehameha Highway (Hwy 83) north of Honolulu near Hauula. Windward shore

Barbers Point Beach Park
West of Honolulu airport up Highway 95. Scuba when surf is low, restrooms

Bellows Beach Park
Twenty miles up the Pali Highway (Hwy 61) then turn on Kalanianaole Highway (Hwy 72)

Blaisdell Beach Park
In Honolulu, east on Highway 99. Southshore, restrooms

Chun's Reef - Kawailoa
Off Highway 83 about 30 north of Honolulu airport at Kawailoa Beach. Exposed north shore

Diamond Head Beach Park
Off Diamond Head Road, across from state park

Ehukai Beach Park
North of Haleiwa off Highway 83. Exposed north shore. Snorkeling good when flat. Restrooms, showers

Ewa Beach Park
Southeast of Ewa off Highway 76. South shore, seasonal high surf. Restrooms

Fort Derussy
At west end of Waikiki. Snorkeling, restrooms

Photo courtesy of Ron Owen

Haleiwa Alii Beach Park
Off Highway 821, 25 miles north of Honolulu airport. Snorkeling, scuba, restrooms, showers

Haleiwa Beach Park
Off Highway 83, 25 miles north of Honolulu airport. Snorkeling, trailer and tent camping, restrooms

Hanauma Bay Beach Park
East of Waikiki off Highway 72. Snorkeling, scuba, restrooms, showers

Hauula Beach Park
North of Honolulu airport off Highway 83. Trailer and tent camping

Hawaiian Electric Beach Park
West of Honolulu airport off Highway 93

Hoomaluhia Park
East of Honolulu off Highway 63. Camping, hiking

Kaaawa Beach Park
North of Honolulu off Highway 83. Camping, snorkeling, restrooms

Kahana Bay Beach Park
North of Honolulu off Highway 83. Trailer camping. Rrestrooms

Kahe Point Beach Park
West of Honolulu off Highway 93. Trailer and tent camping. Snorkeling, scuba, restrooms

Kailua Beach Park
Off Highway 72, 25 miles from Honolulu. Snorkeling, restrooms, showers

Kaiona Beach Park
Off Pali Highway (Hwy 61) and Kalanianaole Highway (Hwy 72). Snorkeling, restrooms

Kalae-oio Beach
Park up windward shore near Kaaawa. Snorkeling

Kaneohe Beach Park
Off Highway 63

Kapiolani Park
In Honolulu walking from Waikiki Beach toward Diamond Head. Aquarium, Honolulu Zoo, Kodak Hulu show. Restrooms, phone

Kaupo Beach Park
Up Pali Highway (Hwy 61) then off Highway 72. Snorkeling

Keaau Beach Park
North of Waianae off Highway 93. Tent and trailer camping. Snorkeling, restrooms

Keehi Lagoon Beach Park
East of Honolulu off Highway 64. Restrooms

Oahu

Diamond Head silhouetted by a golden sky. Photo courtesy of David McCray

Oahu

Koko Head Beach Park
East of Waikili off Highway 72. Scuba, restrooms

Kualoa Point Park
Twenty miles north of Honolulu off Highway 83. Camping, snorkeling, restrooms

Kuhio Beach Park
In Honolulu on the way to Diamond Head off Kalakaua Ave. Restrooms

Kuilei Cliffs Beach Park
East of Honolulu off Diamond Head Rd. Snorkeling

Kuliouou Beach Park
East of Waikiki off Highway 72

Laenani Beach Park
North of Honolulu at Kahaluu. Restrooms

Laie Beach Park
Off windward shore (Hwy 83). Seasonal high surf

Laniakea Beach - Kawailoa
North of Haleiwa off Highway 83. Snorkeling

Lualualei Beach Park
Near Waianae off Highway 93. Camping, restrooms

Maili Beach Park
South of Waianae off Highway 93. Snorkeling, restrooms, showers

Makaha Beach Park
North of Waianae off Highway 93. Camping, snorkeling, restrooms, showers

Makapuu Beach Park
Northeast of Honolulu off Highway 72. Seasonal camping, snorkeling, restrooms, showers

Seasonal Camping
Makua Beach
North of Waianae off Highway 93. Snorkeling, scuba

Mauna Lahilahi Beach Park
North of Waianae off Highway 93. Snorkeling, restrooms

Maunalua Bay Beach Park
East of Waikiki off Highway 72. Snorkeling, restrooms

Mokuleia Beach Park
West of Haleiwa off Highway 930. Trailer and tent camping, snorkeling, restrooms

Nanakuli Beach Park
South of Waianae off Highway 93. Trailer and tent camping, snorkeling, scuba, restrooms, showers

Oneula Beach Park
Southwest of Ewa off Highway 76. Restrooms

Pearl Harbor Park
National Historic Landmark. Restrooms

Pokai Bay Beach Park
At Waianae, west of Pearl City off Highway 93. Excavated heiau (holy place). Snorkeling, restrooms, showers

Punaluu Beach Park
South of Laie off Highway 83. Trailer and tent camping. Snorkeling, restrooms

Pupukea Beach Park
North of Haleiwa off Highway 83 on north shore. Snorkeling, restrooms

Photo courtesy of Cory Gray

Oahu

Iolani Palace, Oahu. Photo by Paul Seaman, courtesy of Hawaii Visitors Bureau

Queen's Surf Beach Park
In Honolulu, across from Kapiolani Park off Kalakaua Ave. Restrooms

Sandy Beach Park
East of Waikiki on Highway 72. Restrooms, showers

Sunset Beach
West of Laie off Highway 83. North shore. Snorkeling

Swanzy Beach Park
South of Laie on Highway 83. Trailer and tent camping, snorkeling, restrooms

Ulehawa Beach Park
South of Waianae off Highway 93. Snorkeling, restrooms

Waiahole Beach Park
Northeast of Honolulu off Highway 83.

Waialae Beach Park
East of Honolulu off Highway 72. Snorkeling, restrooms

Waialee Beach
West of Laie off Highway 83. North shore, snorkeling

Waianae Regional Park
North of Waianae off Highway 93. Snorkeling, restrooms

Waikiki Beach Center
Off Kalakaua Ove in Waikiki. Restrooms, showers

Wailupe Beach Park
Northeast of Honolulu airport off Highway 72. South shore, restrooms

Waimanalo Beach Park
Northeast of Honolulu off Pali Highway (Hwy 61) then up Highway 72. Windward shore, trailer and tent camping, snorkeling, restrooms

Waimea Bay Beach Park
West of Laie off Highway 83. North shore, snorkeling, restrooms, showers

Following page. Statue of King Kamehameha, Oahu. Photo courtesy of the Hawaiian Visitor's Bureau

Diving Oahu

Oahu has diving along all of its shores. Because of the prevailing winds and high surf on the northern sections of the islands during winter months, most of the diving takes place on the western, southern and eastern shores.

Because of excessive street traffic on the island, tour operators serve their customers with hotel pick-up and transportation to the boat-launch sites. Oahu offers a good blend of sites accessible from boats as well as from shore.

Boats are located in Kewalo Basin which, for the most part, take divers up and down Oahu's southern coast. On the leeward shore in Waianae Harbor near the town of the same name, there are also charter boats that will take you out to the wreck of the Maui and other popular Oahu dive spots.

There are a number of good dive spots just a few miles out of Kewalo Basin. Divers board the dive boats next to Fisherman's Wharf in Honolulu. One of the first spots you will run into out of the harbor is **Rainbow Reef**. Comprised of long fingers of lava extending seaward and perpendicular to the shoreline, the water depth ranges between 10 and 35 feet. Expect to see very tame wrasse and angelfish swim up for a handout. Also, closer to the bottom, you'll see moorish idols, eels and a variety of tropicals. One of the newest sites off Waikiki Beach is the 174-foot long **YO257**, sunk in 1989 about a mile offshore as part of the artificial reef system. Known by local divers as the "YO" this wreck was put into place by the Atlantis Submarine operation ([808]522-5801) in order to provide underwater scenery for the passengers in their sub. For this reason the wreck is sometime called the Atlantis wreck. The "YO" is a steel-hulled oiler which is in very good condition with masts, piping and

A new wreck to Oahu is the Hilton wreck off the coast from Waikiki Beach. Photo courtesy of Cory Gray

wheelhouse reasonably intact. In the wheelhouse the helm, still intact, will provide a great prop for taking a few a pictures of your dive buddy. The vessel rests on a flat bottom, upright in about 100 feet of water, with masts that extend to within 40 feet of the surface. In beautiful condition, the wreck already has quite a complement of fish. Expect to find large schools of fish like trumpetfish, Hawaiian balloon fish and bluestriped snapper as well as jacks and tuna. The wreck has many open areas and one very large opening cut out of its hull for easy access and good lighting for photographers.

The unique feature of this wreck is the periodic visits of the Atlantis Submarine. Divers can watch the sub circle the wreck while tourist submariners peer out of their viewing ports. This is a great wide angle photo opportunity for a diver in the right place at the right time.

Also just out of Kewalo Basin by boat is the dive spot The **100 Foot Hole** which was once a royal Hawaiian fishing site. You can still find ancient fishing artifacts here today. There are numerous caverns and caves full of critters like whitetip reef shark, octopus, eels and lobsters. The ancient Hawaiians were smart to fish here because you will also find a lot of game fish at this spot. If you're looking to see a few Hawaiian turtles underwater then dive at **Turtle Canyon**. You can see up to a dozen turtles on one dive. The reef runs about five miles in length with water depth about 30 to 40 feet. The turtles here are so tame they totally ignore divers. This makes for a great place to get good turtle photographs. More turtles can be found under ledges or overhangs. A great beach dive is at **Hanauma Bay**, a white sand beach that is also a very popular snorkeling spot. Part of an extinct submerged volcanic cone which collapsed on one side opened up this crater to the sea. What formed was a natural lagoon, which is rated one of the most beautiful beaches in the state. It is designated as a Marine Life Conservation District and thousands come daily to this spot to swim, snorkel and dive. For an easy snorkel you can stay inside the reef in about 10 feet of water. Move out past the reef and you'll find that the maximum depth runs about 70 feet at the bay's outermost point. There are hundreds of different species of very tame fish.

On the north shore at Pupukea Beach County Park check out a beach dive at **Shark's Cove**. Spearfishing is not allowed inside this cove. You'll be hard pressed to find a shark here despite the name and this is a summer-only beach dive, but in about 45 feet of water you will find many archways and passageways with multiple openings all well lit. Dive around the point on the right side of the bay. As you swim along you will find many

lava tubes and archways. Sea life includes eels and other tropicals. This is the north shore so is not really divable except from May to October. In the winter you have to get lucky with the weather condition. Check with the dive shop. Around the **Kaena Point** on the eastern, leeward shoreline you will find a number of interesting boat

One of the most popular wreck dives off Oahu is the Mahi on the lee side of the island. Photo courtesy of Cory Gray

dives. You can get on a number of boats out of Waianae Harbor. A very popular spot with the dive boat operators is **Makaha Caverns**, a maze of caverns, caves and passageways. Depth ranges between 15 and 50 feet. Here you will find a wide variety of sealife such as pufferfish, hawkfish, trumpetfish, moorish idols, menpachi squirrelfish and the state of Hawaii's fish, the Humuhumunukunukuapau'a. These fish are accustomed to lots of divers as this is a fairly popular spot for the dive boats so they are

all looking for a handout. Nearby is what is probably the island's most popular dive spot, the wreck of the Mahi. The 185-foot long former minesweeper displaces 800 tons. At one point it was a oceanographic research vessel for the University of Hawaii. Sunk in 1982, it sits upright in about 95 feet of water. You may find a strong current here and schools of fish suspended over the wreck. On the main deck the most insistent of the sea life are large schools of lemon butterflyfish and taape. They are obviously used to being fed regularly by divers. You will find morey eels, whitetip sharks and eagle rays and a lot of photo opportunities. Two large sections have been cut from the ship's starboard hull and the aft deck's hold cover and hatches have been removed for easy diver penetration if the current isn't too strong.

Important Phone Numbers

Fire, Police, Ambulance 911

Hyperbaric Treatment Center
42 Ahui St.
Honolulu, HI
(808) 523-9155

Coast Guard
(800) 331-6176

Weather Service
(808) 836-0234

Surf Conditions
(808) 836-1952

Queen's Medical Center
1301 Punchbowl
Honolulu, HI
(808) 538-9011

Kaiser Foundation
1697 Ala Moana Blvd
Honolulu, HI
(808) 949-5811

Diver's Alert Network (DAN)
(919) 684-8111

Diving Oahu

Useful Phone Numbers

Hawaii Visitor Bureau
2270 Kalakaua Ave
Honolulu, HI 96815
(808) 923-1811

Arizona Memorial
(808) 922-1626

Bishop Museum
(808) 922-1626

Honolulu International Airport
(808) 836-1411

Distant Chart Miles

Honolulu-Waikiki Beach 3
Honolulu-Kailua via Nuuanu 13
Honolulu-Kaena Point via Waianae 45
Honolulu-Honolulu Airport 5
Honolulu-Waimanalo via Koko Head 22

Photo courtesy of Cory Gray

Dive Shops & Boats

Name Address, Phone	Reference #	Hour	Affiliation	Compressor	Rentals	Repairs	Comments
Aaron's Dive Shop, Inc 602 Kailua Rd. Kailua, Oahu, HI 96734 (808) 262-2333	001	8am-8pm M-F 7am-6pm Sat 7am-5pm Sun	PADI	3500 psi	Y	Y	
Aaron's Dive Shop, Inc. #2 46-216 Kahuhipa St. Kaneohe, Oahu, HI 96744 (808) 235-3877	002	8am-6pm M-F 7am-6pm Sat Closed Sun	PADI	3500 psi	Y	Y	
Aaron's Dive Shop, Inc #3 Camp Smith Scuba Locker Campsmith, Oahu, HI	003	9am-6pm M-F 9am-5pm Sat Closed Sun					
Aloha Dive Shop Koko Marina Shopping Center Hawaii-Kai Honolulu, Oahu, HI 96825 (808) 395-5922	004	7:30am-5pm Daily	PADI NAUI SSI	3000 psi	Y		
Aquaventure-Turtle Bay 40 W. Kuilima Kahuku, Oahu, HI 96731 (808) 293-8811 ext. 597	005		PADI		Y	Y	
Bojac Aquatic Center 94-801 Farrington Hwy. Waipahu, Oahu, HI 96797 (808) 671-0311	006	9am-6pm M-F 8am-6pm Sat-Sun	NAUI	3500 psi	Y	Y	
Breeze Hawaii Diving Adventures Corp. 3014 Kaimuki St. Hololulu, Oahu, HI 96816 (808) 735-1857	007	7am-6pm Daily	PADI	3000 psi	Y	Y	
Dan's Dive Shop 660 Ala Moana Blvd. Honolulu, Oahu, HI 96813 (808) 536-6181	008	8am-4pm Daily	NAUI PADI	3000 psi	Y	Y	
Down Under Divers 94-866 Moloalo, Bldg. B-13 Waipahu, Oahu, HI 96797 (808) 671-1065	009	9:30am-6pm M-F 7:30am-6pm Sat-Sun	INS NAUI	3500 psi	Y	Y	
Hawaii Sea Adventures 98-718 Moanalua Rd. Pearl City, Oahu, HI 96782 (808)487-7515	010	Everyday	PADI	3500 psi	Y	Y	
Leeward DiveCenter 87-066 Farrington Hwy. Maili, Oahu, HI 96792 (808) 696-3414 (800) 255-1574	011	7:30am-6:30pm Daily	PADI 5-Star	3500 psi	Y	Y	
Oahu School of Diving and Pro Dive 95 S. Kamehameha Hwy. Wahiawa, Oahu, HI 96786 (808) 622-2283	012		NAUI PADI	3500 psi	Y	Y	

Dive Shops & Boats

Name, Address, Phone	Reference#	Hour	Affiliation	Compressor	Rentals	Repairs	Comments
Rainbow Divers 1640 Wilikina Dr. Wahiawa, Oahu, HI 96786 (808) 622-4532	013	9am-6pm M-F 8am-6pm Sat-Sun	PADI 5-Star	3500 psi	Y	Y	
South Seas Aquatics 870 Kapahulu Avenue #109 Hololulu, Oahu, HI 96816 (808) 735-0437	014	8am-6pm Daily	PADI 5-Star	3000 psi	Y	Y	
South Seas Aquatics 2155 Kalakaua Center Suite 112 Waikiki Beach, Oahu, HI 96815 (808) 922-0852	015	10am-9pm Daily	PADI 5-Star	3000 psi	Y	Y	
Surf & Sea 62-595 Kam. Highway Haleiwa, Oahu, HI 96712 (808) 637-9887	016	9am-6pm Daily	PADI	3000 psi	Y	Y	
Waikiki Diving Center 1734 Kalakaua Ave. Hololulu, Oahu, HI 96826 (808) 955-5151	017	8am-6pm Closed Sun	PADI NAUI	3500 psi	Y	Y	
Vehon Diving Ventures Hawaii-Kai Shopping Center Honolulu, Oahu, HI 96825 (808) 396-9738	018	8am-5pm Daily	PADI NASDS	3200 psi	Y	Y	
Dive Oahu P.O. Box 173 Kahuku, Oahu, HI 96731 (808) 293-1187	A						Charter Boat Only
Divestar of Hawaii 94-1139 Polinahe Pl. Waipahu, Oahu, HI 96797 (808) 677-7337	B						Charter Boat Only
Elite Dives Hawaii 67-239 B Kahaone Loop Waialua, Oahu, HI 96791 (808) 637-9331	C						Charter Boat Only
First Dive Tours, Inc. 2301-A Waiomao Rd. Honolulu, Oahu, HI 96816 (808) 732-6972	D						Charter Boat Only
Ocean Adventure, Inc. 98-406 Kamehameha Hwy. Pearl City, Oahu, HI 96782 (808) 487-9060	E						Charter Boat Only
South Seas Aquatic 1050 Ala Moana Blvd. Honolulu, Oahu, HI 96814 (800) 252-6244 (808) 538-3854	F						Charter Boat Only
Steve's Diving Adventures 1860 Ala Moana Blvd. Honolulu, Oahu, HI 96815 (808) 947-8900	G						Charter Boat Only

Dive Shops & Boats

Name, Address, Phone	Reference#	Hour	Affiliation	Compressor	Rentals	Repairs	Comments
Waikiki Diving, Inc. 420 Nahua Street Hololulu, Oahu, HI 96815 (808) 922-7188	H						

DIVE SPOTS

	Dive Spots	Depth	Expertise	Boat or Beach Dive
Rainbow Reef	(100)	10-30 feet	All levels	Boat
YO257	(101)	100 feet	Intermediate	Boat
The 100-foot Hole	(102)	80-100 feet	Intermediate Advanced	Boat
Turtle Canyon	(103)	15-40 feet	Intermediate	Boat
Hanauma Bay	(104)	10-110 feet	All levels	Beach
Shark's Cove	(105)	20-60 feet	All levels	Beach
Makaha Caverns	(106)	15-50 feet	All levels	Boat
Mahi	(107)	100 feet	Intermediate	Boat

Photo courtesy of Cory Gray

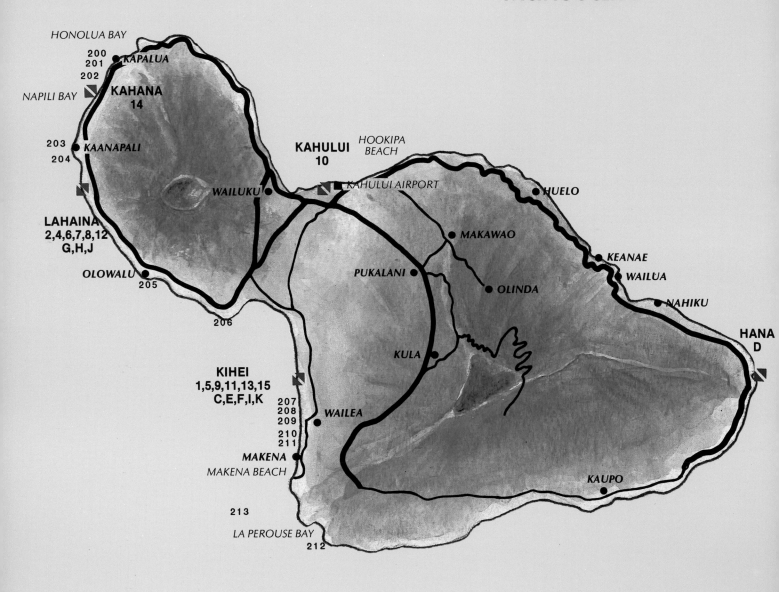

PACIFIC OCEAN

HONOLUA BAY

200
201
202 ● *KAPALUA*

NAPILI BAY ◰ **KAHANA**
14

203 ● *KAANAPALI*
204

◰ **LAHAINA**
2,4,6,7,8,12
G,H,J

OLOWALU ●
205

206

KIHEI
1,5,9,11,13,15
C,E,F,I,K ◰

207
208
209 ● *WAILEA*
210
211

MAKENA ●
MAKENA BEACH

213

LA PEROUSE BAY
212

KAHULUI
10

HOOKIPA BEACH

◰ *KAHULUI AIRPORT*

WAILUKU ●

HUELO ●

● *MAKAWAO*

PUKALANI ●

● *OLINDA*

KEANAE ●
WAILUA ●

NAHIKU ●

KULA ●

HANA
D ◰

KAUPO ●

PACIFIC OCEAN

PACIFIC OCEAN

THIS MAP IS NOT TO BE USED
FOR NAVIGATIONAL PURPOSES

Maui
The Valley Isle
With Lanai, Molokai and Kahoolawe

The islands of Maui, Lanai, Molokai and Kahoolawe collectively form the county of Maui. Originally formed volcanically as one enormous island, the region later subsided, flooding the basin now separating the four islands with warm Pacific waters. Of these four islands, Maui captures the majority of the tourist population. The other islands boast a more pristine and traditionally laid back Hawaiian atmosphere.

The island of Maui is the center of diving activity in Maui County. Most of the exceptional diving lies along the shoreline of Lanai, Molokai and Molokini Crater, a small volcanic dimple a few miles off Maui's southwest shoreline. The dive spots off these nearby islands are inaccessible, except via one of the charter boats that operate out of Maui. Daily trips are scheduled out of Kihei, Wailea and Lahaina on Maui. Kahoolawe is used for gunnery practice by the Navy and is off limits.

Exploring Maui

Most people's first exposure to this region is on Maui at the island's largest airport in the central town of Kahului. The town is located at the northern entrance of a deep valley that runs south through the center of Maui. Outlined by waterfalls and white sand beaches, this valley is the passage-

Statue of Buddha at Jodo Mission. Photo courtesy of Cory Gray

way that connects both coastlines and exists at the most narrow portion of the island.

Much of the major sightseeing on Maui radiates outward from Kahului. For example, about 5 miles to the west where Highway 32 dead ends is the **Iao Valley**. There surrounded by cliffs thousands of feet high, its slopes carved steeply by water, stands one spectacular spire that has resisted time and erosion. The Iao Needle rises to a height of 2,250 feet above the valley floor.

Also out of Kahului, a few miles up the northern coastline along Highway 340, is the old, rustic town of Wailuku where you can explore the **Maui Historical Society Museum**. To the east of Kahului winding along the rugged northern coast is the **Road to Hana**. Waterfalls and deep valleys cut into this mountainous terrain; black sand beaches punctuate the isolated fishing villages and old lava flows. The jungle is dense and filled with mango and monkeypod trees. Coffee plants, bamboo, ferns and African tulip trees create a forest with every imaginable shade of green coupled with that blue, blue ocean where deep Pacific water meets volcanic rock. This is the car ride of a lifetime! The trip to Hana is on a long, narrow road (figure one whole day) but well worth the trouble.

The island of Maui originates from two large volcanos separated by a long, beautiful, lush green valley. The larger volcano, **Haleakala Crater**, rises 10,023 feet above the ocean. Located on the eastern region of the island it is the largest crater in the world (see Haleakala). The trip up Highways 377 and 378 to the crater takes you through beautiful, wooded landscape where horse trails wind up the crater's steep sides and meander across its moon-like surface. This is a terrain that lends itself to horseback riding which is very popular in this region

Lanai is a favorite dive destination for charter boats operating on Maui. Photo courtesy of Rick Baker

of Maui. At the rim of the crater, scientists at the observatory study the stars. These facilities are not open to the public. Bike riding tours that start at the crater's rim and wind down the steep road to the base are available.

For scuba divers, most of the action is on the southwestern coast. For thousands of years sailing vessels used this coastline for protection from the harsh Pacific. The town of **Lahaina** was once the royal capital of Maui and is preserved to retain much of the flavor of a century ago. The islands Molokai, Lanai, Kahoolawe and Maui form a protected rectangle of water. This region, if circled on a map, encompasses the best of Maui diving with few exceptions.

In hidden and protected coves along the shoreline between La Perouse and Kaanapali is the area with the finest beach diving on Maui. Most of the charter services for divers are in Lahaina or Kihei. Along these leeward shores you'll find an abundance of snorkeling and SCUBA diving facilities. You can rent gear, book a boat dive or learn how to snorkel or dive.

In contrast, the northern shoreline has some attractive dive sites, but most are remote and slightly exposed. The southeast shore is subject to high surf and strong currents and is off limits for divers. Roads in these areas are hazardous.

The islands of Lanai and the Molokini crater offer the scuba diver spectacular offshore diving. These dive spots are all accessible to scuba divers on half and full day boat trips.

One more bonus for divers on Maui is the whales. Every year playful humpbacks migrate from the polar region to warm **Maalaea Bay** to spend the winter. There is even a chance you may see one underwater or hear that unmistakable sound that only a humpback whale makes.

The Elite Too runs charters off the lee side of Oahu. Photo courtesy of Rick Baker

Getting There

The Kahului Airport on Maui accommodates 9 different airlines, with more than 90 flights a day. From Los Angeles or Dallas you can fly *American Airlines* daily. Flights on *United Airlines* will deliver you to Hawaii direct from Chicago, Los Angeles or San Francisco. Daily charters booked by *Suntrips* fly from San Francisco aboard *Hawaiian Air* and *Ward Air* operates weekly flights from Canada.

From Honolulu to Maui, Molokai or Lanai, *Hawaiian Air* or Air Molokai offer daily flights. *Aloha Airlines* also serves Maui from Honolulu. This flight lasts 18 minutes. Once on the island of Maui, you can pick up a *Gray Line Hawaii* shuttle at Kahului Airport that will take you to the west side resort areas like Kaanapali Beach. Taxis to the west side of Maui run $20 and up. *Air Molokai*, a relatively small airline, flies aircraft like the twin-engine Cessna into the smaller airports on Molokai

and Lanai. There is also a ferry service to these remote islands leaving Lahaina, Maui, daily.

Most people will want to rent a car while visiting the Hawaiian Islands. On Maui take a shuttle to the car rental depot. Car rental prices are very competitive here. In a few minutes you're off to your hotel. Divers with a lot of gear will find it a relief to arrive at one of the "outer island" airports. The distances you have to haul your gear are short compared to Honolulu Airport.

Visitor Information: (808) 872-3894

Staying There

Maui offers a price range for everyone's budget. For example, the traveling diver can stay in the Pioneer Inn ($50-$70/night) in Historic Lahaina where the majority of dive operations are within walking distance, or stay 10 miles away at the several very luxurious resorts at Kapalua, Kaanapali, and Wailea ($130 and up). Maui is the land of the golf course and most of the big resorts have their own golf courses as well as tennis courts and swimming pools.

Many of the dive operations on Maui cooperate with the local hotels in the area and have put together some very attractive packages for divers.

If you really want to save some money, renting a condo is the way to go. A moderately priced condo ($50-75/night) has a fully equipped kitchen and laundry. If quiet is your thing then find a condo a few miles out of Lahaina to the north on the old Honoapiilani Road. Here, right on the beach, you will enjoy semi-private beaches, swimming pools and a snorkeling reef offshore. There is an abundance of quiet and a wonderfully warm breeze. The drive into Lahaina to restaurants, shops, movie theater or diving charter services is about 5-

The view of Lanai from the shores of Maui. Photo courtesy of David McCray

10 minutes and there are some good dive spots locally right offshore.

Camping & Hiking

There are 31 federal, state and county parks on the island of Maui. Of all the parks with campsites, none is located near Maui's best diving on the West Coast. Most are on the rugged and windy northern coastline off the Hana Highway or up on the Haleakala Volcano.

Maui tent camping in designated County and State Parks requires permits. Cabins are available in State Parks and Haleakala National Park. Reservations are necessary for these accommodations, as advance permits may be required.

There are also some nice campgrounds on the more remote islands of Molokai and Lanai. See the sections on those islands for more details.

On Maui hiking trails zig-zag across the whole island. Some of the best spots to set out on foot and explore are in the crater on Haleakala, on the southwest end around Hana and some short outings around the Iao Needle (See Haleakala and Iao Needle in this chapter).

Parks
STATE PARKLANDS

Division of State Parks, Maui Dist.
54 High St.
P.O. Box 1049
(808) 244-4354
Wailuku, HI 96793
(Permits good for up to 5 nights)

Haipuaena Recreation Site
Off of Hana Hwy(Hwy 360). Hiking, no drinking water (Contact Division of Forestry and Wildlife).

Halekii-Pihana Heiau State Monument
In Wailuku, off of Hwy 340. No drinking water.

Iao Valley State Monument
Four miles west of Wailuku at end of Iao Valley Road (Hwy 320). Botanical gardens, Iao Needle, restrooms.

Kanaha Bird Sanctuary
Junction of 36 and 37. Observation Hut (Contact Division of Forestry and Wildlife).

Kaumahina State Wayside (camping)
Off the Hana Hwy (Hwy 360). Beautiful exotic plants, some nice sight seeing. Camping (no showers), restrooms.

Keanae Arboretum
Off Hwy 360. Hiking, no drinking water (Contact Division of Forestry and Wildlife).

Launiupoko State Wayside
On West Coast, south of Lahaina on Hono-a-Piilani Hwy (Hwy 30). Small beach park – picnicking, swimming, restrooms.

Maui

Papalaua State Wayside
On Maui's west coast on the Hono-a-Piilani Hwy(Hwy 30). Fishing, picnicking, snorkeling, swimming. No drinking water.

Poli Poli Spring State Recreational Area (camping)
Off Hwy 377 in Kula Forest Reserve. 4-wheel drive advised. Tent camping, no showers, hiking, picnicking, restrooms, grills. One cabin available.

Puaa Kaa State Wayside
On Hana Hwy (Hwy 360). Rain forest. Picnicking, swimming restrooms, grills, shelters.

Puohokamoa Recreational Site
Off the Hana Hwy (Hwy 360). Hiking, picnicking, no drinking water or restrooms (Contact Division of Forestry and Wildlife).

Wahikuli State Wayside
North of Lahaina on Hono-a-Piilani Hwy (Hwy 30). Canoeing, fishing, picnicking, restrooms, outdoor showers, stoves.

Waianapanapa State Park
East of airport off the Hana Hwy (Hwy 360). Tent and trailer camping, fishing hiking picnicking, swimming, restrooms, outdoor showers (camping).

Photo courtesy of Rick Baker

Waikamoi Recreation Site
East airport off Hana Hwy(Hwy 360). Hiking, spring water drinking fountain. No restrooms. (Contact Division of Forestry and Wildlife).

Wailua Valley State Wayside
Off Hana Hwy (Hwy 360). No drinking water.

COUNTY PARKS
County Parks Department
Kaahumanu Ave
War Memorial Center
Wailuku, HI 96793
(808) 244-9018
(For County Parks you only need a permit to camp in Baldwin Beach Park)

Baldwin Park (camping)
Off Hana Hwy(Hwy 360). Tent camping, picnicking, swimming, restrooms, shelters.

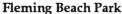

Fleming Beach Park
North of Lahaina off Hwy 30. Picnicking, swimming, restrooms, grills, shelters.

Hana Beach Park
Off main highway at Hana. Picnicking, restrooms, grills, shelters.

Hanakaoo Beach Park
North of Lahaina on Hwy 30. Picnicking, swimming, restrooms, grills.

Honokowai Beach Park
North of Lahaina on Hwy 30. Picnicking, restrooms, grills.

Hookipa Beach Park (camping)
East of airport on Hwy 360 (Road to Hana). Tent camping, picnicking, restrooms, grills, shelters.

Kalama Beach Park
South of Kihei on Kihei Rd. Picnicking, swimming, restrooms, grills, shelters.

Kalepolepo Beach Park
South of Kihei on Kihei Rd. Picnicking, restrooms, grills.

Kanaha Beach Park
North of airport off Hwy 380. Picnicking, swimming, restrooms, grills.

Photo courtesy of Rick Baker

Kepaniwai Park
West of Wailuku on Hwy 320. Heritage gardens, stream. Picnicking, swimming (pool), scenic viewing, restrooms, grills, shelters.

Maipoina Oe lau Beach Park
South of Kihei on Kihei Rd. Picnicking, swimming, restrooms, grills, shelters.

Paunau Park
South of Lahaina on Hwy 30. No drinking water.

Rainbow County Park
East of airport via Highways 36 and 390. Camping, picnicking, restrooms.

Waiehu Beach Park
North of airport off Hwy 340 at Waiehu. Picnicking, restrooms, grills, shelters.

Waihee Beach Park
North of airport off Hwy 340 at Waihee. Picnicking, restrooms, grills.

Federal/National Parklands
P.O Box 369
Makawao, HI 96768
(808) 572-9306

Haleakala National Park
Head for the top of the volcano on Highways 36 to 37 to 377 to 378. At

the visitor center inquire about camping, hiking, horseback riding, nature study, picnicking, swimming. Cabins in crater by reservation. Free crater tent camping available daily on first come first serve basis. Cabins are reserved by monthly lottery. Send requests with preferred and alternate days to address listed above. No permits needed at Hosmer Cove or Oheo Gulch for tent camping.

Sea turtles are common in the Hawaiian Islands. Photo courtesy of Rick Baker

HALEAKALA

To the southeast of Maui's famous garden valley filled with lush vegetation and tall waterfalls looms the volcano Haleakala. The drive up the mountain will take a few hours, but the narrow road comprised of many switchbacks seems to build anticipation as you approach the crater at the top. Erosion has played a major part in the barren, lunar-like landscape that exists inside Haleakala's huge crater. A national park since 1916, its last eruption was in 1790. It was at this time that the crater floor was filled with cinders and cinder cones. Most scientists now consider Haleakala dormant.

The mountain is 10,023 feet above sea level at a spot called Red Hill in the crater which measures 3,000 feet deep, 7.5 miles long and 2.5 miles wide. The tallest cinder cone, Puu o Maui, stands 500 feet above the crater floor.

Haleakala is a Hawaiian word that means "House of the Sun." A trip to the top of this mountain reveals where it got its name. On Maui, amid the lush vegetation and waterfalls, it is easy to forget these Hawaiian Islands were volcanically formed. This landscape quickly reminds us that we are all sitting on a giant volcano.

Watching the sun rise over the eastern rim is an experience described by visitors as unforgettable. Bike excursion companies will get you up in the early hours of the morning and drive you up to see the sunrise. This spectacular event is followed by a most exhilarating bicycle ride down the volcano.

Hikers may explore the crater on several trails, but park rangers warn that the high, thin air can cause light-headedness and headache. Wear warm clothing that can be removed in layers — weather conditions can be sunny one minute and cold and rainy the next. After a day of diving in 80 degree water in tropical weather, it's hard to imagine cold winds and rain. Bring extra clothes. If you have been doing a lot of diving, it is a good idea to wait 12 hours before driving up to the top of a 10,000 foot mountain.

For those who just want to take a look around, the park has a House of the Sun Visitor Center with a great view of the crater. The visitor center is open from sunrise to 3 pm; the park is open 24 hours a day. Fifteen minute talks on park geology and natural history are given three times a day. A 2-½ hour crater hike on the Sliding Sands Trail in the crater is offered at 10 a.m. every Saturday. Meet at the visitor center. The park entrance fee is $3 per car. For more information call (808) 572-9306.

The last volcano to erupt on Maui was Haleakala. It is the largest crater in the world. Photo courtesy of Rick Baker

Iao Valley State Monument

This needle-like rock formation rising 2,200 feet above the valley floor of the Iao Valley State Park is the result of erosion. Originally part of the West Maui volcano, the needle was once a portion of a long ridge. The ridge wore down on either side of the needle leaving a saddle-shaped formation. The rock that became the needle was harder for rain water to erode because it was originally part of a volcanic "plug." This "plug" filled a channel that connected with the main magma chamber of the volcano deep in the earth.

So say scientists from the West, but Hawaiian legend has its own theory. According to legend, Maui, a powerful god of the island, had a daughter named Iao. Maui and his wife Hina were so taken by their child that they discouraged her participation in activities enjoyed by other girls her age.

Admirers, fearing the anger of Maui, didn't dare pursue Iao, who was forced to be contented with daily visits to the beach to pass the time.

Then one day, at a pool near her house, she met Puuokamoa, a merman god of the pool, who was transformed into a man when he met Iao.

When Maui found out, he captured the merman and sentenced him to death, but the volcano goddess Pele convinced him to make Puuokamoa a permanent reminder of what can happen when you defy sacred law.

Puuokamoa's fate was sealed. He was turned into a pillar of stone, rising from the mountains west of Wailuku.

To reach this attraction, drive from Wailuku on High Street (Hwy 30) to the intersection where the road becomes Iao Valley Road.

Important Maui Phone Numbers

Ambulance, Fire Department, Police
911

Coast Guard Rescue Center Group Operations Center
(800) 552-6458

Coast Guard Station Maui Search & Rescue Line
(808) 244-5256

DAN (Divers Alert Network)
(919) 684-8111

Hawaii Visitor Information Service
P.O. Box 330002 – Dept. DAHI
Kahului, Maui 96733
(808) 877-4636
(800) 445-INFO

Maui Memorial Hospital
221 Mahalani St.
Wailuku, Maui 96793
(808) 244-9056

Maui Visitors Bureau
250 Alamaha St., Suite N-16
Kahului, Maui 96732
(808) 871-8691

Marine Weather
(808) 877-3477

Weather Forecasts
(808) 877-5111

Mileage Chart Miles

Lahaina–Kapalua	14	Kahului–Haleakala	26
Lahaina–Maalaea	14	Kahului–Hana	52
Lahaina–Kaanapali	4	Kahului–Kihei	10
Lahaina–Kihei	20	Kahului–Wailea	17
Lahaina–Wailea	27	Kahului–Maalaea	12
Lahaina–Wailuku	21	Kahului–Lahaina	22
Lahaina–Kahului	22	Kahului–Kaanapali	27
Lahaina–Haleakala	50	Kahului–Kapalua	37
Lahaina–Hana	76	Kahului- Ulupalakua	24
Kahului–Wailuku	5		

Iao Needle rises 2,250 feet above the valley floor. Photo courtesy of Cory Gray

Visit Our Exclusive Underwater Address.

Kealakekua, the "pathway of the god", is a spectacular natural marine reserve considered to be one of the best dive and snorkel spots in Hawaii. This protected harbor offers spectacular marine life, coral reefs, underwater rock formations and lava tubes.

Fair Wind is privileged to moor in this historic, protected bay. You can share the beauty and discoveries of our ocean paradise with your entire family aboard our custom, 50–foot trimaran. Enjoy scenic cruising along the Kona Coast, swimming, snorkeling, diving, sunning on spacious decks, water sliding, and viewing the abundant variety of colorful tropical fish through our on-board glass bottom.

A Family Adventure You'll Not Soon Forget!

Fair Wind's many activities will provide enjoyment for everyone. We offer two cruises daily, with a full BBQ lunch on our morning cruise, and snacks on our afternoon cruise. Come aboard and let us treat you to a memorable adventure.

- Includes snorkel gear and professional instruction
- SCUBA equipment available
- Whale watching in season
- Family owned and operated for over 20 years

For information, call toll-free:
800-872-4341 ext.4
(in Hawaii: 322-2788)

78-7128 Kaleiopapa St.,
Keauhou Bay ,Kona, Hawaii 96740

FAIR WIND

WHERE YOU'RE ONE OF OUR FAMILY

Diving Maui

The submerged basin outlined by the islands Maui, Molokai, Lanai and Kahoolawe on a map forms a giant playground for scuba divers. Along the perimeter and within these boundaries is some of the best diving in the Hawaiian Islands.

The dive spots off the shores of Lanai and Molokai are accessible to divers mainly via one of the charter dive boats whose home ports dot the west coast of Maui. It would seem logical to stay on Molokai or Lanai to dive these prize dive locations but because of the absence of good roads on these remote islands these spots are more accessible from the boats on Maui. Dive stores and boats have a hard time surviving on these remote islands. As of this writing there are no dive stores or dive shops on either Molokai or Lanai.

To dive safely in the Hawaiian Islands requires knowledge of currents and weather patterns. Currents can be tricky offshore and it is best to always dive with someone who knows the area. Getting information from one of the local dive stores on Maui as to the best place to dive is always a good idea. As a matter of fact, this is a good rule of thumb when diving anywhere in the Islands.

Maui has some great beach diving. It is very easy to drive into Lahaina to one of the many dive shops, rent some gear and be in the water within the hour. Maui has a very out-of-the-way low key atmosphere and diving off the beach is no exception. But the Maui charter boats usually choose locations in Molokini Crater, Lanai or

Lahaina was once the royal capital of Maui. Today a number of charter boats moored in the harbor transport divers to many of the nearby islands. Photo courtesy of Rick Baker

Molokai. For more information on these spots see the sections on Lanai and Molokai in this chapter.

The island of Kahoolawe (which is owned by the Navy and used for gunnery practice) is off limits to tourists, dive boats and divers.

Along the coast of Maui most of the best beginner diving is along the protected West Coast region. On the slightly exposed northwest perimeter of this region is **Honolua Bay**. There is good wall and reef diving on both sides of the bay. The coral reefs there host wrasses, triggerfish, eels, puffers, moorish idols, goatfish, surgeonfish, turtles, manta rays and butterflyfish. You will find that the best time of year to dive this area is during the spring and summer months. In the

winter large waves frequently roll in. Get latest conditions from your local dive shop before heading up the coast to dive here. The shallow area is great for beginners and snorkelers. Another dive spot exposed to larger seas is **Mokuleia Bay** but when the water is calm this area is very popular with snorkeler, scuba diver and body surfer alike. It is a little difficult hiking down to the beach with all your gear but once you're in the water, head out to either side of the point and you will find reef fish, coral, and a lava flow! Summer months are the only time to dive this exposed area. Once again, it is a good idea to talk to the people in the local dive stores for information on sea conditions. **Kapalua Bay** has public access at the left end of the beach with a rocky point on the right side of the bay. Enter as close to the point as you can and follow the point out into deeper water. Outside of the bay are rock ledges covered with sea urchins and coral heads. Snorkelers will love these waters too. Black Rock is a small enclosed bay with a large underwater lava formation covering the sea floor. This is part of the reason the visibility at this spot can be so exceptional. It is located just off shore from the Sheraton Hotel on Kaanapali Beach. Park in the Sheraton parking lot and walk through the complex to the beach. Swim around the point into the submerged cinder cone. Great night dive location because the visibility is good and also because the volcanic bottom topography helps divers keep their bearings in the dark. **Hyatt Reef,** named for the Hyatt Regency Resort at Kaanapali Beach, is a densely-packed coral formation cut by sand channels that run perpendicular to the shoreline. Look for butterflyfish, goatfish, yellowtail coris and small trivially jacks and sea turtles. If you swim seaward you will find some huge antler corals. **Olowalu** is equally superb for snorkeling and diving. Water is shallow with large fields of finger corals dotting the underwater landscape. Dive boats carefully navigate in here when all other dive spots are blown out. Look for sea turtles, octopus, crown-of-thorns starfish and the occasional manta ray. At **Papawai Point** park at the scenic lookout parking lot, walk down the trail to the beach. Like the plaque at the head to the trail says, this is a favorite site for whale watching. During the winter months you can hear them underwater! At **Keawakapu Beach** snorkelers and divers will find an artificial reef installed in 1957. This

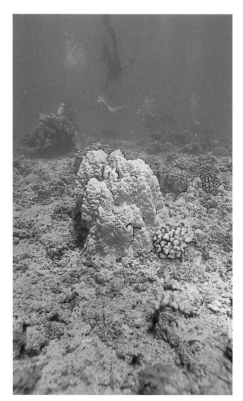

Coral heads are plentiful under Hawaiian waters. Photo courtesy of Rick Baker

Photo courtesy of Cory Gray

reef has helped to develop a substantial fish population in this area. **Ulua** and **Mokapu** are two beaches good for snorkeling and scuba. There is parking plus restrooms and showers. Enter on the beach and go find the volcanic reef that extends out from the point. **Wailea Beach** is also a sheltered place for the beginner snorkeler to the advanced diver with rocky points at each end of the beach. Swim to one of the points and then follow the reef into deeper water. Polo Beach off the town of Wailea is a good place to snorkel when the water is calm. Swim out to the lava flow that comprises the point. At **Haloa Point** head out and around the wash rocks and find a spectacular reef packed with sea life, including ray, eels and even a few turtles. **Five Graves** near La Perouse Bay is a popular site south of Kehei which is often visited by dive operators out of Kihei and Makena. This spot is also accessible from the beach. Park your car in the small cemetery. Extending out from the Nahuna Point is a large reef with underwater caves along the northern drop off in about 30 feet of water. Look for the resident white tip shark. Pinnacles rise from the bottom and crimson sponges cover a site call **Red Rock.** **La Perouse Bay** is bisected by a seaward running ridge. Look for the red slate pencil sea urchins.

    Molokini Crater is a partially submerged volcanic crater with a 400-yard section of the crater rim ascending above the surface of the water. The only way to get to and dive this crater is by boat. The critters here are protected by the State Marine Life Conservation District. Within the crater walls are colorful coral formations, schools of lemon

Lahaina, Maui. Photo courtesy of David McCray

Diving Maui

butterfish and jacks. This is a well protected spot great for snorkelers and divers alike. The depth range is from ten to 100 feet.

On the backside of the crater a gentle current will carry you along a steep drop-off where large white-tip sharks cruise at depth. Manta and eagle rays are also encountered at this dive spot. The bottom is at 350 feet. Schooling tuna and dolphins seem to emerge from the deep crevices.

Reefs End is an extension of the rim of the northwest tip of the crater. In deeper waters are ledges where many species of eel reside. Look for moray, dragon, snowflake and garden eels. At the other tip of the Molokini crescent is a spot similar to Reefs End which is called Shark Ledges.

Most the time, diving along the southern and eastern shores of Maui is hampered by waves created by the almost daily occurrence of the easterlies. When they are not blowing, usually in the winter, there is some good diving on these shores. There is also a nasty south swell that crops up occasionally. Dive these spots using extreme caution and always with the knowledge and experience of someone who knows the area. Use good judgment.

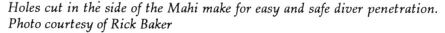
Holes cut in the side of the Mahi make for easy and safe diver penetration. Photo courtesy of Rick Baker

Dive Shops & Boats

Name, Address, Phone	Reference#	Hour	Affiliation	Compressor	Rentals	Repairs	Comments
Bill's Scuba Shack 36 Keala Place Kihei, Maui, HI 96753 (808) 879-3483; (800) 950-3483	001	7am - 6pm Daily	PADI	3300 psi	Y	Y	
Captain Nemo's 150 Dickenson St. Lahaina, Maui, HI 96701 (800) 367-8088; (808) 661-5555	002	7am - 9pm Daily	PADI 5-Star	3500 psi	Y	Y	
Central Pacific Divers 780 Front St. Lahaina, Maui, HI 96761 (800) 551-6767; (808) 661-8718	003				Y		
Dive Maui Inc. 900 Front Street #J6 Lahaina Center Lahaina, Maui, HI 96761 (808) 667-2080	004	9am - 9pm Daily	NAUI PADI SSI	3300 psi	Y	Y	Sales, rentals, boat dives.
The Dive Shop of Kihei, Ltd. P.O. Box 917 2411 S. Kihei Rd. Kihei, Maui, HI 96753 (808) 879-5172	005	8am - 5pm Daily	PADI 5-STAR	3000 psi	Y	Y	
Extended Horizons P.O. Box 10785 Lahaina, Maui, HI 96761 (808) 667-0611	006		PADI NAUI				Private instruction
Hawaiian Reef Divers 129 Lahainaluna Rd Lahaina, Maui, HI 96761 (808) 667-7647	007	8am - 6pm Daily	PADI NAUI	3300 psi	Y	Y	Charters, dive store, sales, , instruction.
Lahaina Divers 710 Front St Lahaina, Maui, HI 96761 (800) 551-6767 (808) 667-7496	008		PADI 5-STAR NAUI SSI	3500 psi	Y	Y	Dive boat, boat charters, sales, instruction.
Maui Dive Shop Azeka Place Kehei, Maui, HI 96753 (808) 879-3388	009	8am - 9pm M-Sat 8am - 6pm Sun	PADI 5-STAR	3000 psi	Y		
Maui Dive Shop 279 Wakea Ave. Kahului, Maui, HI 96732 (808) 871-2111	010	9am - 5pm M-Sat Closed Sun	PADI 5-STAR	3000 psi	Y	Y	
Maui Dive Shop Kihei Town Center Kihei Maui, HI 96753 (808) 879-1919	011	8am - 9pm Daily	PADI 5-STAR		Y		
Maui Dive Shop Lahaina Cannery Lahaina Maui, HI 96761 (808) 661-5388	012	9am - 9pm Daily	PADI 5-STAR		Y		
Maui Dive Shop Kamaole Shopping Center Kihei Maui, HI 96753 (808) 879-1533	013	7am- 9pm Daily	PADI 5-STAR		Y		

Dive Shops & Boats

Name, Address, Phone	Reference#	Hour	Affiliation	Compressor	Rentals	Repairs	Comments
Maui Dive Shop Gateway Shopping Center Kahana, Maui, HI 96761 (808) 669-3800	014	8am - 8pm Daily	PADI 5-STAR		Y		
Maui Sun Divers P.O. Box 565 Kihei, Maui, HI 96753 (808) 879-3631 (808) 879-DEEP (800) 747-DIVE	015		NAUI	3300 psi	Y		Charters, instruction, rentals. Specialize teaching and beach diving.
Central Pacific Divers 515 S. Kihei Rd. Kihei, Maui, HI 96753 (808) 874-0884	A						Charter Boats Only
Central Pacific Divers The Plantation Inn 174 Lahainaluna Rd Lahaina, Maui, HI 96761 (800) 433-6815	B						Charter Boats Only
Ed Robinson's Diving Adventures P.O. Box 616 Kihei, Maui, HI 96753 (808) 879-3584; (800) 635-1273	C						Charter Boats Only
Hana Bay P.O. Box 481 Hana, Maui, HI 96713	D						Charter Boats Only
Makena Coast Charters P.O. Box 1599 Kihei, Maui, HI 96753 (808) 874-1273	E						Charter Boats Only
Mike Severns Scuba Diving P.O. Box 627 Kihei, HI 96753 (808) 879-6596	F						Charter Boats Only
Sundance Scuba Charters P.O. Box 12491 Lahaina, Maui, HI 96761 (808) 667-2842	G						Charter Boats Only
Pacific Dive Services Inc. 277 Wili Ko #21 Lahaina, Maui, HI 96761 (808) 667-5331	H						Instruction
Scuba Hawaii 1325 S. Kihei Rd., Suite 114 Kihei, Maui, HI 96753 (808) 874-1001	I						Charter Boats Only
Scuba Schools of Maui 1000 Limahana Place P.O. Box 11328 Lahaina, Maui, HI 96761 (808) 661-8036	J						Sales, instructions.
Steve's Diving Adventure 1993 Kihei Rd. Suite 22 Kihei, Maui, HI 96753 (808) 879-0055	K						Charter Boats Only

Dive Spots

	Dive Spot	Depth	Expertise	Boat or Beach Dive
Dive Spots Maui				
Honolua Bay	(200)	10-45 feet	All levels	Beach
Mokuleia Bay	(201)	10-50 feet	Intermediate Advanced	Beach
Kapalua Bay	(202)	10-45 feet	All levels	Beach
Black Rock	(203)	15-25 feet	All levels	Beach
Hyatt Reef	(204)	35-40 feet	All levels	Boat
Olowalu	(205)	10-30 feet	All levels	Beach
Papawai Point	(206)	35-60 feet	All levels	Beach
Keawakapu Beach	(207)	10-35 feet	All levels	Beach
Ulua & Mokapu	(208)	10-45 feet	All levels	Beach
Wailea Beach	(209)	10-40 feet	All levels	Beach
Haloa Point	(210)	10-45 feet	All levels	Beach
Five Graves (Nahuna Point)	(211)	45-60 feet	Advanced	Beach
La Perouse	(212)	10-65 feet	Intermediate Advanced	Boat
Molokini Crater	(213)	10-130 feet	Inside crater All levels Outside crater Intermediate Advanced	Boat
Dive Spots Lanai				
Hulopoe Bay	(215)	10-50 feet	All levels	Beach
The Cathedrals	(216)	35-60 feet	Intermediate Advanced	Boat
Second Cathedrals	(217)	20-70 feet	All levels	Boat
Sergeant Major and Sergeant Minor	(218)	35-45 feet	All levels	Boat
Knob Hill	(219)	20-70 feet	Intermediate Advanced	Boat
Lighthouse Reef	(220)	15-65 feet	All levels	Boat
Shark Fin Reef	(221)	15-75 feet	Beginning Intermediate	Boat
Dive Spots Molokai				
Mokuhooniki Rock	(214)	20-100 feet	Advanced	Boat

Side Trips from Maui

MOLOKAI

For years this island was known as "The Lonely Isle" which originally referred to the leprosy victims exiled here in the last century. Today this quiet, easy-going town screams of "old Hawaii." It only takes a few minutes to see why its new name, "The Friendly Isle," applies. Molokai is still considered an Hawaiian island that is "off the beaten path." Not a single traffic light exists within the boundaries of this 38 mile long by 10 mile wide island. At least half the island's 6,700 residents are of Hawaiian ancestry. This means that Molokai can boast the state's largest assembly of native Hawaiians.

Like all the other Hawaiian Islands, Molokai's terrain is rich with diversity. Just like the other islands there is a dry, flat west end and a windswept jungle-like east side with the world's largest sea cliffs ascending to heights of 3,000 feet or more.

Take a hike up the Halawa Valley on the trail to Moaula Falls. The 2-½ mile hike will be rewarded with a plunge in the deep pool at the base of the 250-foot high Moaula Falls.

Also a treat are the guided horseback rides and tours to Iliiliopae Heiau which is considered one of Hawaii's largest and best preserved temples. For the serious hikers, the Nature Conservancy, (808) 567-6680, can arrange access to the Kamakou rain forest and Moomomi Dunes, nesting site for the endangered Hawaiian green turtle. Here you will also find a research site for Hawaiian prehistory, paleontology and geology. For more information write:

Destination Molokai
Travel Sales Ltd.
1600 Kapiolani Blvd. Suite 923
Honolulu, Hawaii 96814
(800) 367-ISLE

Hidden in a branch of black coral a small Long–nosed Hawkfish. Photo courtesy of Cory Gray

The Kalaupapa Peninsula

This National Historic Park encompasses 10,000 acres and was established in 1980 to commemorate the leprosy colony founded at Kalawao in 1866. The colony was moved to Kalaupapa in 1888 when a water pipeline was installed there. You can book a tour to the former leprosy colony of Kalaupapa by plane, mule or foot. Access is limited to 100 people a day so reservations are mandatory.

The mules are sure-footed but if you have a fear of heights you might want to hike the trail for $30/person. The 6-½ hour long mule ride down the three mile long Kalaupapa Trail costs $85 per person. A ten minute plane ride can also be booked at $70 per person. All these prices include lunch and a tour.

At the bottom of the cliff you board a mini-bus for the settlement. No one is allowed to roam unattended. The tour includes small wooden houses, medical facilities, Father Damien's church, Mother Marianne's memorial and graveyards.

For more information contact: Molokai Mule Ride (800) 843-5978, Damien's Molokai Tours (808) 567-6171 or Kalaupapa National Historical Park (808) 567-6102.

Getting There — Staying There

Molokai Airport is serviced by daily commuter flights from Lanai, Maui and Oahu. There is a daily ferry service from Lahaina, Maui.

Molokai's accommodations are limited to a few condominiums, a low-rise resort and a couple of small hotels.

At the full service Kaluakoi Hotel and Golf Club on and at the adjacent Kaluakoi Villas, Paniolo Hale and Ke Nani Kai condominiums at the west end of the island, you will pay between $85 and $200 a night. Contact the Activity Director at the hotel to line up private scuba diving tours on the island.

In Kaunakakai, the Pau Hana Inn with beach front bar features local bands and an enthusiastic hometown crowd. Here the rates start at $45 a night. Nearby and also in this price range is the Hotel Molokai.

Molokai Parklands

Palaau State Park
P.O Box 526
Kaunakakai, HI 96748
3 miles northeast of Kualapuu off Hwy 470. Camping, hiking, picnicking.

County Parklands

Maui County Dept. of Parks and Recreation
P.O. Box 526
Kaunakakai, HI 96748
(808) 553-3221

Halawa Park
At Halawa, east of airport at end of Kamehameha Hwy (Hwy 450). Hiking trail, waterfalls, plunge pool, swimming, restrooms.

One Alii Beach Parks 1 and 2
At One Alii, southeast of airport on Hwy 450. Camping, picnicking, swimming, fishing, restrooms, showers.

Papohaku Beach Park
At Kalua Koi, west of airport. Camping, fishing, picnicking, swimming, restrooms, showers.

PACIFIC OCEAN

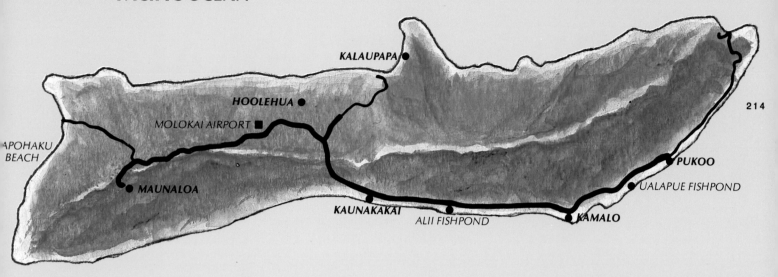

KALAUPAPA

HOOLEHUA

MOLOKAI AIRPORT

214

APOHAKU
BEACH

PUKOO

MAUNALOA

UALAPUE FISHPOND

KAUNAKAKAI

KAMALO

ALII FISHPOND

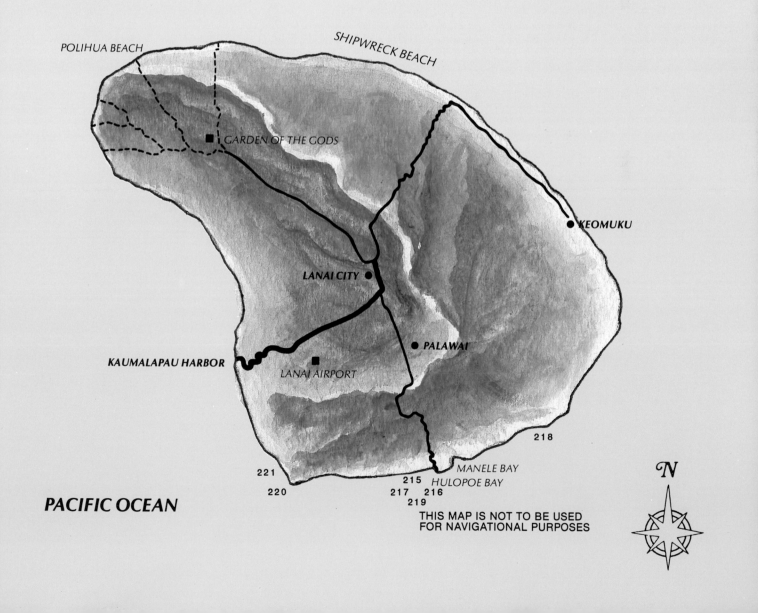

POLIHUA BEACH

SHIPWRECK BEACH

GARDEN OF THE GODS

KEOMUKU

LANAI CITY

KAUMALAPAU HARBOR

PALAWAI

LANAI AIRPORT

221

218

220

MANELE BAY

215   216

HULOPOE BAY

217   219

PACIFIC OCEAN

N

THIS MAP IS NOT TO BE USED
FOR NAVIGATIONAL PURPOSES

Diving Molokai

MOLOKAI

Currents around Molokai are considered tricky and treacherous even to the locals and many of the beaches are closed to the public. There are no dive shops or resorts on Molokai that cater directly to scuba divers but on the west end of the island at the newly built Kaluakoi Hotel and Golf Club the activity director can set you up with a local guide who can take you out on his boat for the day. These trips are expensive but very personalized. Equipment is supplied, but it might be a good idea to bring your own regulator.

If you are staying on Maui or Oahu, many of the charter boat services on these islands do one day and multi-day trips to Molokai, eliminating the inconvenience of getting around the island. The most popular dive destination is **Mokuhooniki Island** off the east end of the island. The best time of the year to dive Molokai is between May and September. If you are going to beach dive ask the local folks at your resort about current conditions, directions or if a guide is available.

At the **Kaluakoi Hotel and Golf Club** there is great snorkeling on the reef offshore where you will find a broad assortment of reef fish. **Mokuhooniki Island** is accessible only by dive charter from Maui or Oahu and is only divable about 25 days of the year when the ocean is extremely calm. Eagle and manta rays, hammerhead sharks and large schools of goatfish, pennantfish, pyramid butterflyfish and blue striped snapper can be found close in to shore.

The pineapple industry is still the main economy on Lanai. Photo courtesy of Bill Shofstall

Diving Lanai

Just a few thousand people live on this quaint and rural island called the "Pineapple Island." Most of the people of Lanai are involved in one way or another with pineapples, but this is changing with the recent growth in the tourist population. With just three paved roads, travel about the island can best be described as rugged and 4-wheel drive vehicles are recommended in many area. If you get stuck, even finding a phone can sometimes be a challenge.

In the center of the island, on a 1600 foot high plateau, is Lanai City, the only town on the island and where most of the people live. Nestled at the foot of Lanaihale Mountain, this small town hosts a small runway with daily flights from the other islands. The Hotel Lanai, the only hotel in town and one of two hotels on the whole island, is the town's tourist center. The two-story soon to open Lodge at Koele will increase the island's hotel count to three.

The tourist industry is just starting to grow on Lanai. Lack of roads and the position of the island restricts the divable beaches to one or two. In some areas, a 4–wheel drive vehicle is required. For these reasons most of the diving is done by charter boats from Maui which visit the dive spots along the protected southwest shore of Lanai.

One of the few fairly accessible beach dives on Lanai is **Hulopoe Bay**. This spot is a favorite with the natives. Also visited by dive boats, its numerous arches and reef are host to numerous fish posed over a most colorful reef.

From a charter boat from Maui, Lanai offers a multitude of dive

Photo courtesy of Cory Gray

Until recently, the Hotel Lanai was the only hotel on the island. Photo courtesy of Bill Shofstall

Diving Lanai

spots along its southwest shoreline. The visibility often exceeds 100 feet. Two separate dive spots make up **The Cathedrals**. These two connecting grottos are on the inside of a massive underwater ridge. Shafts of light beam down openings from above to illuminate a rear wall, giving the larger cavern a "cathedral-like" appearance. The holes and pockets in the volcanic rock on the wall and ceilings are filled with schools of menpachi squirrelfish, solitary "big eye" squirrelfish and slipper lobsters.

The **Second Cathedrals** is a series of connected grottos within a large pinnacle which juts upward from 60 feet. The cathedral floor rests at about 55 feet. Huge arches and columns meet you at the main entrance. Here you will find a few lobsters, shrimp, eel and other creatures hiding in small crevices and caves along the sides of the main rooms. Around the outside of the pinnacle, divers will confront pyramid butterflyfish, moorish idols and bluestriped snappers.

Down the coast of Lanai are more dive locations. **Sergeant Major** and **Sergeant Minor**, named for a series of parallel ridges, are located east of the First Cathedrals. Here, in 40 feet or less, divers can explore caves, tunnels and arches or swim with large green turtles. **Knob Hill** is another popular dive site. On the south shore of Lanai are more caves and archways formed by a huge lava formation. Two ridges radiate outward into deeper water. Along these ridges you will find octopuses, scorpionfish, moray eels and raccoon butterfish.

Around the southwest corner of Lanai is **Lighthouse Reef** which is protected by a short natural breakwater. A small archway rests on the bottom at about 25 feet where a vertical wall drops to a gently slop-ing coral bottom in 20-30 feet of water. In the lava tubes you will fine small white-tip sharks, some puffers, a multitude of "candy cane" shrimp and Hawaiian lobsters. **Shark Fin Reef** is just north of Lighthouse Reef. A long narrow ridge runs perpendicular to shoreline; there are also arches, walls, submerged pinnacles and caves to explore. Scorpionfish, octopuses three times a day.

In Lanai City you can rent 4-wheel drive vehicles, cars and pickup trucks. For prices and availability call Lanai City Service (808) 565-6780.

At this point there are two hotels on Lanai. The Hotel Lanai in Lanai City (808) 565-7211 and the Manele Bay Hotel (808) 565-7700. Almost completed is the Lodge at Koele.

The backside of Molokini crater has a wide variety of sea life like this Liopard Blenny. Photo courtesy of Cory Gray

and various small morays are regularly encountered on the rugged bottom.

Getting There — Staying There

Hawaiian Airlines and Air Molokai serve Lanai from Honolulu and Maui daily except on Saturday. A daily ferry service out of Lahaina, Maui, called Expeditions (808) 661-3756, travels to Manele Bay

Camping

There are six campsites on the island all at Hulopoe Beach. Showers, toilets and water are available. For information write:

Koele Co.
Box L
Lanai City, HI 96763
(800) 565-6661

Travel Companies

Destination Hawaii
932 Ward Ave., #490
Honolulu, HI 96814
(800) 359-6201

More Hawaii for Less
5324 Kester Ave., #4
Van Nuys, CA 91411
(800) 367-5108

Tourist Activity Center
Ocean Activity Center
1325 So. Kihei Rd., #212-A
Kihei, Maui, HI 96753
(808) 879-4485

Ghost shrimp photographed on the back side of Molokini crater. Photo courtesy of Cory Gray

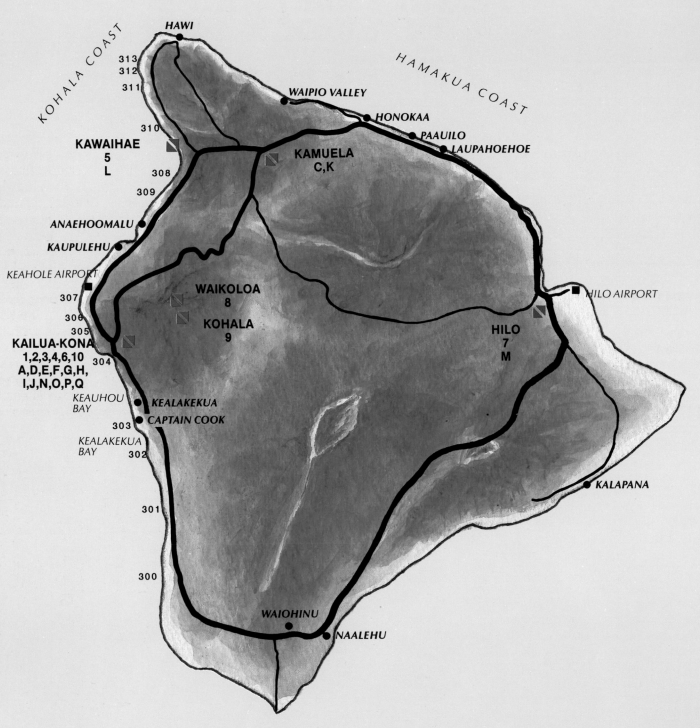

HAWI

KOHALA COAST

HAMAKUA COAST

313
312
311

310

WAIPIO VALLEY

HONOKAA

KAWAIHAE
5
L

308

309

KAMUELA
C,K

PAAUILO

LAUPAHOEHOE

ANAEHOOMALU

KAUPULEHU

KEAHOLE AIRPORT

307

WAIKOLOA
8

KOHALA
9

HILO AIRPORT

306

305

KAILUA-KONA
1,2,3,4,6,10
A,D,E,F,G,H,
I,J,N,O,P,Q

304

HILO
7
M

KEAUHOU
BAY

KEALAKEKUA

CAPTAIN COOK

303

KEALAKEKUA
BAY

302

301

KALAPANA

300

WAIOHINU

NAALEHU

PACIFIC OCEAN

THIS MAP IS NOT TO BE USED
FOR NAVIGATIONAL PURPOSES

HAWAII
The Big Island

As your plane makes its final bank, lining up with the small runway at Hawaii's Keahole Airport, take a casual glance out the window at the rugged, primitive terrain. Geologically this island is still forming, which is one of the reasons the landscape is unique in the Hawaiian Islands. Sharp, black volcanic rock protrudes skyward, enclosing the small airport. There is no doubt you are on a volcano and for a short period of time you're going to be one of its inhabitants. Throughout your visit, both on land and underwater, you will constantly be reminded of this island's volcanic origins.

On land, one of the most obvious reminders is the erupting volcano Mauna Kea. Underwater, you will notice the still young (compared to the other islands that formed earlier geologically) coral reefs are undeveloped and thinly cover the black volcanic ocean bottom. In many ways, both above and below water, nature hasn't had enough time on this island to disguise this volcanic terrain with its veil of life. As you move north, the islands get older and the flora and fauna get denser and more complex.

Nicknamed the Big Island, Hawaii is the largest of all the Hawaiian Islands. About 4,000 miles square, Hawaii is twice the size of all the other islands in the whole chain put together. In addition, this island has the distinction of being one of the biggest islands in the Pacific Ocean.

Actually this island is composed of five volcanos, not all of which are active. These volcanos are named Kohala, Hualalai, Mauna Kea, Mauna Loa, and Kilauea. These mountains rose from volcanic activity that is still going on today and which began on the seafloor south of Maui. Eventually rising to the sea's surface, these five volcanos created what we today call the island of Hawaii. Mauna Kea is known as the world's largest seamount because it rises 20,000 feet up from the seafloor to sea level then 13,796 feet above sea level. Of all these volcanos only Mauna Loa and Kilauea are presently active. Different from volcanos on the mainland, magma here flows down the mountain in small rivers of molten rock rather than exploding, like Mount St. Helens did. This makes the spectacular lava fountains relatively safe to watch.

The major tourist development is centered around Kailua-Kona near the airport. Here you will find dive stores and dive boat operations. The beaches along the Kona Coast are very volcanic with jagged, sharp irregular rocks making most of the dive spots accessible strictly by boat. But once you're in the water, diving here is consistently good some 350 days of the year.

Black volcanic rock is exposed everywhere on this obviously volcanic island.
Photo courtesy of David McCray

Hawaii—The Big Island

Exploring The Big Island

At the southernmost tip of the Hawaiian chain, the Big Island has a very quiet, out-of-the-way atmosphere. This is partly because of its fresh volcanic landscape that seems to also transport you back through time to the days of the early Hawaiians. You can still find villages untouched by the modern world. Standing in one of the historically preserved Hawaiian villages you will find yourself day dreaming of the lives of the men and women who lived there hundreds of years ago.

The Big Island offers black volcanic beaches, recently cooled and still steaming lava flowing at the base of active volcanos, snow-covered mountains with dry, arid deserts at the base of their flanks, and lush tropical forests nestled in deep V–shaped valleys encircled with waterfalls.

Hawaii is also rich in history. You can see homes of the first missionaries to land on this island, reconstructed Hawaiian heiau (holy place), ancient royal palaces and America's only coffee plantations.

The variety of activities range from snow skiing to marlin fishing. This island has more parks, campgrounds and hiking trails than any of the other islands. Contact the Visitors Bureau for information about your favorite activity.

There is so much to do and see on this island that you should leave at least a day for each side of the island (east and west side). The island is so large that getting around either end of the island from Kailua to Hilo or vice-versa will take most of the day, and that is pushing it. To really tour the island you should spend a few days in Hilo, then move your base of operation to Kailua and explore this rapidly growing region of the island.

The Saddle Road

There are three basic ways to get to and from these two towns. The most direct route is along the "saddle road." This passes through a valley that lies between the two largest volcanos on the island: Mauna Kea and Mauna Loa. The road is a little rough in a few spots, but is paved the whole way. This extremely rugged, volcanic region is said to resemble the face of the moon. Up here you can stay at one of the cab-

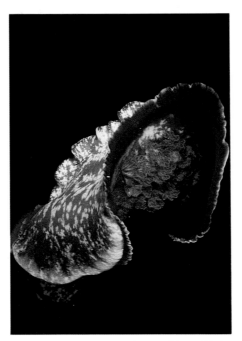

Spanish Dancer caught on film off the Kona Coast. Photo courtesy of Cory Gray

ins in the Mauna Kea State Park. It's a great place to stay if you're on your way to the summit as a hiker or skier.

The Kohala Coast

There are two other roads from Kailua to Hilo that take the coastal route around the northern and southern parts of the island. To the north you drive up Highway 19 which intersects with Highway 270. That road will follow the shoreline to the Kohala Coast. Along this route you will find some of the nicest resorts on the island. North of Puako is the Hapuna State Recreation Area with one of the most beautiful and biggest white sand beaches anywhere. Many restored historical Hawaiian heiau's (holy places) dot the coast and at the Lapakahi State Historical Park there is a 600 year old restored Hawaiian fishing village. At the tip of the island near Upolu you will find the birth site of **King Kamehameha**.

From Upolu Point you can take route 250 into Waimea where you can visit the Parker Ranch. Continue on Highway 190 to the Honokaa coast and on into Hilo. Along this route in Honokaa you will find an interesting macadamia nut factory. From there head up Highway 240 to the Waipio Valley Lookout. From here you can hike what is probably one of the most beautiful, completely enclosed and remote valleys on the island. It's a mile wide, and from the lookout you can see streams, thousand foot high waterfalls and a black sand beach. From the lookout you can hike down on a 6 mile long trail and explore this beautiful spot.

The Kona Coast

Heading south out of Kailua you will find your way along the Kona Coast on Highway 11. Turn left at the **Kealakekua Bay** sign heading downhill toward the ocean. Soon you will reach the town of **Napoopoo** and at the end of the road, park your car. On the hill above you is Mauka, the preserved **Hikiau Heiau**, a Hawaiian holy place dedicated to the god Lano. This is the site of one of the first meetings of Hawaiians and Europeans which occurred in 1778 when Captain Cook

Replica of Hawaiian village at the Puuhonua O Honaunau National Historical Park on Kona Coast. Photo courtesy of Rick Baker

Black sand beach at Kaimu on the windward side of the island. Photo courtesy of David McCray

sailed into this bay. Across the bay is a monument to the great explorer which marks the spot where he was killed a month later. From Kealakekua Bay you can take the bumpy road that runs along the coast to Puuhonua O Honaunau. This National Historical Park is a restored Hawaiian village which was at one time considered a holy place by the natives. There is a visitor center where you can get a brochure for a self-guided tour. This is also one of the all time great places to snorkel on Hawaii. To get back to Highway 11 head up the main road on Rt. 160.

Visiting an Active Volcano

One of the biggest tourist draws on the island is the Hawaii Volcanos National Park where the active volcanos Mauna Loa and Kilauea can be found 30 miles south of Hilo down Highway 11. At the edge of the park you will run into the Kilauea Visitor Center. Of the two active volcanos, Kilauea is presently the one erupting. Encircling Kilauea is a road called Crater Rim Drive. This is the only drive through volcano in the world. About 11 miles long, this stretch of road gives you an overview of the park's major attractions. You will see the visitor center and markers along the trail will guide you to the hiking trails in the area. If the volcano is erupting, the ranger at the visitor center will guide you to the safest place to view the eruption.

Also along Crater Rim Drive is the Volcano House, the oldest hotel on the island, dating back to the 1860's. Here you can get lunch or dinner or book a room for the night at the edge of an active volcano.

Getting There

Jumbo jets land at the General Lyman Field which is the largest and only international airport on Hawaii. On the western and opposite side of the island is the Keahole Airport, a much smaller and much more convenient destination for divers who plan to stay in Kona. Both airports have car rental agencies and taxi service. You can also find restaurants, information centers, shops and lockers. From Keahole Airport the Grayline can take you into Kailua for under $10.

United Airlines has two non-stop flights (one from Los Angeles, the other from San Francisco) that fly into Keahole Airport. Island carriers including Hawaiian Air, Aloha Airlines and offer daily flights from Honolulu, Kauai, Holokai, Lanai and Maui to both Hilo and Kona.

Keahole Airport (808) 329-2484
General Lyman Field (Hilo)
(808) 935-0809

Hawaii — The Big Island

Staying There

Because most of the charter boats and dive shops are centered along the Kona Coast operating out of Honokohau and Kailua Harbors, it is most convenient for divers to stay in this area. A number of large hotels and condominiums can be found along this coastline between Kailua-Kona and Keauhou Bay.

The other major concentration of hotels and condominiums is in Hilo and along the Kohala Coast. On the Kohala Coast there are some of the most luxurious hotels on the island.

Camping & Hiking

To get information on camping and hiking on the island of Hawaii, visit the National Park Headquar-ters across from the Volcano House. One possible diversion is a hike to the top of Mauna Loa. There are two free cabins available – one at 10,000 feet and the other at the summit– but you must sign up in advance. There are also hiking trails around the Volcano House. Contact the Hawaii National Park listed below. At the state parks, cabins rent for about $8 a night. Information on these parks and where you can rent camping gear is also listed below. Advance permits may be required so call for information.

Camping Rental Equipment:
Pacific United Rent All
1080 Kilauea Ave.
Hilo, HI
(808) 935-2974

Kona Rent All
74-5602 Alapaa St
Kailua-Kona
(808) 329-1644

STATE PARKLANDS
Division of State Parks, Hawaii District
P.O. Box 936 or 75 Aupuni St.
Hilo, HI 96721-0936
(808) 961-7200
Permit required for camping.

Akaka Falls State Park
At end of Akaka Falls Rd.
(Hwy 220). Hiking.

Hapuna Beach State Recreation Area
A few miles south of Kawaihae off Queen Kaahumanu Hwy (Hwy 19). Camping, scuba diving & snorkeling, surfing. Restroom and showers.

The smoldering crater on Hawaii is still very much active. Photo courtesy of David McCray

Hawaii—The Big Island

Kalopa State Recreation Area
Southeast of Honokaa, end of Kalopa Rd, three miles inland. Camping, hiking, picnicking.

Kamehameha I Birth Site State Monument.
Southwest of Upolu airport off Upolu Airport Rd off of Hwy 270.

Kealakekua Bay State Historical Park
In Napoopoo at end of Beach Rd. (See Side Bar)

Kealakekua Bay State Underwater Park
In Napoopoo at end of Beach Rd.

Kilauea State Recreation Area
South of Hilo on Hwy 11. Hiking.

Lapakahi State Historical Park
North of Kawaihae on Hwy 270.

Early Hawaiian mock settlement. Marine preserve. Scuba diving and snorkeling, restrooms.

Lava Tree State Monument
A few miles southeast of Pahoa (Hwy 132). Picnicking.

MacKenzie State Recreation Area
One Hwy 137, 9 miles northeast of Kaimu. Tent camping, hiking.

Manuka State Wayside
West of Naalehu on Hwy 11. Camping.

Mauna Kea State Recreation Area
West of Hilo on Hwy 200. Cabins, picnicking.

Mookini Heiau State Monument
Southwest of Upolu airport on dirt road off Airport Rd. Historic landmark.

Old Kona Airport State Recreation Area
North of Kailua Pier at end of Hwy 11. Scuba diving, snorkeling. Restrooms, showers.

Wailoa River State Recreation Area
Downtown Hilo, at end of Piilani St. Visitor center, walking, picnicking. Restrooms.

Wailuku River State Park
In Hilo off Waianuenue Ave. Water falls.

COUNTY PARKLANDS
Hawaii County Dept of Parks & Recreation
25 Aupuni St.
Hilo, HI 96720
(808) 961-8311
Permit required for camping, fee charged.

Hawaiian village near Cook Monument. Photo courtesy of Rick Baker

The majority of diving is off the leeward side of the island on the Kona Coast. Photo courtesy of Rick Baker

H.K. Brown Beach Park
South of Hilo off Hwy 130. Camping, snorkeling. Restrooms, showers.

Carlsmith Park
East of Hilo off Kalanianaole Ave., at Keaukaha. Snorkeling. Restrooms, showers.

Glenwood Park
Southwest of Hilo off Hwy 11. Picnicking, restrooms.

Isaac Hale Beach Park
Southeast of Pahoa off Hwy 132. Camping, snorkeling. Restrooms.

Hookena Beach Park
South of Kailua off Hwy 11. Snorkeling. Restrooms, showers.

Kahaluu Beach Park
South of Kailua on Alii Dr. Scuba diving, snorkeling. Restrooms, showers.

Kaimu Beach
South of Hilo off Hwy 130. Picnicking.

Kapaa Beach Park
Northwest of Waimea off Hwy 270. Camping, snorkeling. Restrooms, showers.

Kaumana Caves
West of Hilo off Kaumana Dr. Picnicking, restrooms.

James Kealoha Beach Park
Near downtown Hilo off of Kalanianaole Ave. Camping, picnicking, snorkeling. Restrooms, showers.

Keokea Beach Park
North of Waimea off Hwy 250. Camping. Restrooms, showers.

Kolekole Beach Park
North of Hilo on Hwy 19. Camping. Restrooms, showers.

Laupahoehoe Beach Park
North of Hilo on Hwy 19. Camping. Restrooms, showers.

Leleiwi Beach Park
Near Hilo on Kalamianaole Ave. Snorkeling. Restrooms, showers.

Liliuokalani Gardens
Near Hilo off Manono St. Picnicking. Restrooms.

Magic Sands Beach
South of Kailua on Alii Drive. Restrooms, showers.

Mahukona Beach Park
Northwest of Waimea off Hwy 270. Camping, scuba diving, snorkeling. Restrooms, showers.

Miloii Beach Park
South of Honaunau off Hwy 11. Camping, snorkeling. Restrooms.

Napoopoo Beach Park
South of Kailua off Hwy 11. Restrooms, showers.

Onekahakaha Beach Park
East Hilo off Kalanianaole Ave. Camping, snorkeling. Restrooms, showers.

Punaluu Beach Park
South of Hilo off Hwy 11. Camping. Restrooms, showers.

Slate pencil sea urchin at LaPerouse Pinnacle. Photo courtesy of Cory Gray

Hawaii—The Big Island

Reeds Bay Beach Park
Southeast of Hilo off Kalanianaole Ave.
Snorkeling. Restrooms, showers.

Richardson Ocean Park
East of Hilo on Kalanianaole Ave. Snorkeling. Restrooms, showers.

Spencer Beach Park
North of Keahole airport off Hwy 270.
Camping, scuba diving, snorkeling.
Restrooms, showers.

Waikaumalo Park
North of Hilo off Hwy 19.
Restrooms.

Waiohinu Park
South of Hilo off Hwy 11. Restrooms.

Waipio Valley Lookout
North of Hilo by way of Hwy 19. End of Hwy 240. Restrooms.

Whittington Beach Park
South of Hilo off Hwy 11. Camping.
Restrooms, showers.

FEDERAL PARKLANDS

Hakalau Forest National Wildlife Refuge
Hawaiian and Pacific NWRs
P.O. Box 50167 or
300 Ala Moana Blvd.
Honolulu, HI 96850
(808) 541-1201
On Keanakolu Road drive 12 miles northwest of Hilo.

Hawaii Volcanoes National Park
Hawaii National Park
HI 96718
(808) 967-7311
Southwest of Hilo on Hwy 11 about 30 miles.

Kaloko Honokohau National Historical Park
Puuhonua o Honaunau
P.O. Box 129
Honaunau, HI 96726
(808) 328-2326
North of Kailua-Kona on Queen Kaahumanu Hwy (Hwy 19).

Puuhonua o Honaunau National Historical Park
P.O. Box 129
Honaunau, HI 96726
(808) 328-2326 (808) 328-2326
Take Hwy 160 south of Kailua 19 miles.

Puukohola Heiau National Historical Park
P.O. Box 4963
Kawaikai, HI 96743
(808) 882-7218
Off Hwy 270, south of Kawaihae.

Photo courtesy of Rick Baker

Diving Hawaii

Just about all the diving off the Big Island is found on its west side, known as the Kona Coast. Over 80 miles long, it offers more than 40 different dive sites. Some of the best visibility (100-150 feet) can be found here. This is because of the newly-formed volcanos (about half a million years old): Mauna Loa (13,677 feet) and Mauna Kea (4,093 feet) that shelter this world class dive spot from both wind and wave. Water temperature averages about 78 degrees year round.

Also on this protected lee side of the island is the town of Kailua which is the center of most dive operations. Most of the dive boats can be found in the nearby harbors of Honokohau and Kailua-Kona. From these harbors, many dive locations require less than 30 minutes travel time. Most spots are best accessed from a boat, but there are some great beach dives and snorkeling spots along this coast.

One aspect that distinguishes this dive area from the other islands is the presence of large pelagics. These are free swimming oceangoing critters and they can get quite large. They are common along this coast because of the sharp drop-off relatively close to shore that invites the large pelagics like giant manta rays, yellow-fin tuna, hammerheads or large schools of dolphin. An encounter with one of these critters can change your life. Also, due to the relatively young volcanic rocks on the island, there are many lava tubes, caves

Every sunset is spectacular in the islands. Photo by Bill Romerhaus, courtesy of the Hawaii Visitors Bureau

and tunnels.

The hard volcanic seafloor is clearly exposed here. Because the island is so young, coral hasn't had enough time to develop extensively so it is thinly spread across the ocean's bottom. Lava flowing into the sea has trapped gases which produced many of the un-

Goby on wire coral. Photo courtesy of Cory Gray

derwater features such a caverns, caves, tunnels and cracks. Because this is such a volcanically young area, there are more lava tubes here than anywhere else in the Hawaiian Islands. These tubes are formed as the outside of a lava flow cools, thickens and turns into a crust. The inside portion of the lava continues to flow downward. Soon the

source of the molten rock is cut off and the tube drains, leaving a hard tube behind. Lava tubes extend from the flanks of the volcano right down into the water sometimes for hundreds of feet.

Laeokamini Point has two dive spots, Three Room Cavern and Two Story Caves. Three Room Cavern can be accessed at the entrance in about 40 feet of water. Inside there are three chambers lined with all forms of lobsters, shrimp, moray eels, yellow sponges and nudibranchs. This is one of the most extensive cave systems in the islands. At Two Story Caves you will find two large caverns stacked on top of each other. A hole in the floor of the first cavern leads to the lower level.

At **Honaunau Bay** you will find the **Puuhonua O Honaunau National Historical Park**. Here you can explore a restored Hawaiian village, relax, picnic and then snorkel or scuba. This is one of the best snorkel/dive spots on the island with a coral reef and loads of tropical fish. You can dive shallow water just off the lava rock near the boat ramp or kick out a little farther to the 100 foot plus drop-off. Take 160 off Highway 11 south of Kailua about 20 miles. Enter at the park entrance. It was in Kealakekua Bay that Captain James Cook met his end when thousands of Hawaiians attacked and killed the great navigator. The plaque that marks the spot where Cook fell is at the north end of the bay and is a favorite spot frequented by snorkel boats out of Kailua-Kona Harbor. Also a scuba destination, this end of the bay is nicknamed "The Aquarium" and is filled with very tame fish accustomed to being fed. Look for parrotfish, butterflyfish and white spotted balloonfish. This northern end of the bay is fairly hard to get to except by boat, but the southern corner of the bay is accessible by car. To get there take Highway 11 south to Kealakekua Bay and turn left. Keep driving through Napoopoo until you reach the end of the road. Enter at the bottom of the steps. Water depth ranges 20-35 feet and the bottom is covered with volcanic formations and coral. The swim across the bay to the Cook Monument is long and there is considerable boat traffic in the area. **Red Hill** is actually a number of dive spots in one location. These dive spots have names like **Long Lava Tube, Ridges, Driftwood Caverns, Paradise Cave** and **Amphitheater**. These spots are located between Keikiwaha and Keawakaheka Points and have names that describe the volcanic topography of each area. This overall area was formed when a cinder cone was eroded and divers can find many caves, caverns with skylights and ridges with arches and tunnels. Whitetip sharks can be found in these caves.

Old Airport is a great shore dive just a short distance from Kailua north on Kuakini Street at the old airport. You can enter north or south of the runway. If you enter at the north end there is a protected cove at the end of the parking lot. To access the south end, park at that end of the runway and follow the trail down to the water.

The drop-off, which drops to 100 feet or more, is not far from shore. Exploring the wall will reveal parrotfish, surgeonfish and tangs. On the opposite side of the cove at the north end of the runway you will find an arch. At the south side there is a blow hole connected to the sea by a lava tube. Enter with

caution; if there is any surf, there will be a strong surge.

Kiawi Point is very well protected and one of the most frequently visited dive spots off the Kona coast. Just north of Kailua in less that 20 feet of water you will find numerous caves and archways. Look for the

Diver returning to dive boat. Photo courtesy of Rick Baker

small whitetip sharks, harlequin shrimp, pipefish and octopuses. Coral covers the entire ocean bottom. If you move into deeper water and peek over the drop-off you will see lots of jacks and an occasional manta ray.

At Pine Trees there is a series of about 12 dive sites all uniquely formed by lava. And there is an added attraction: a green turtle with a lot of character. Named "Miss Piggy" by locals, she is always looking for a handout. One of Pine Trees dive spots, called Golden Arches, has two archways and a pinnacle that rest in about 50 feet of water. These volcanic fea-

tures reach upward to within 15 feet of the surface. Another spot in this area is called the **Pinnacles**. Lava tubes, overhangs and archways are packed with sea life. Moving seaward to the edge of the drop-off at about 50 feet you will find large, friendly white mouth eels, yellow margin morays and octopus. A very popular dive spot is the airplane wreck off of **Keahole Point**. **Puako** is an excellent beach dive accessible by car and has an easy entry. This spot is known for it superb visibility. To get there take Highway 19 north from Kailua for 30 miles. At the sign that says Puako, turn left and head for the ocean, continue past the paved road about 25 yards and park. Enter the water at the parking lot. You'll see caverns and an archway near shore plus a shallow drop-off. Lots of turtles and coral here. Off the northern tip of Anaehoomalu Point there is a lava formation named **Pentagon** for the five openings leading to a common cavern inside. A shallow dive at about 25 feet, this spot is great for wide angle photography. Whitetip sharks and spotted eagle rays are common. **Keikei Caves** has an abundance of life which includes eels, pufferfish and butterflyfish. Coral and volcanic rock mix to form small ridges honeycombed with caves and tunnels with depths ranging between 25 and 65 feet. Four major caverns are connected in spots by lava tubes. Sun penetrates into an above-water chamber at **Horseshoe Canyon**. This chamber is found at the end of an 100 foot long lava tube which extends into shore.

A great spot for snorkelers is the **Lapakahi State Historical Park** where you can see lots of coral and the water stays shallow a considerable distance from shore. Great way to spend part of a day. Make sure you take a walk through the restored Hawaiian village. This is

Diving Hawaii

one place where you can really get a feeling of prehistoric Hawaii. **Mahukona Beach Park** can be appreciated by snorkeler and scuba diver alike. Take Highway 19 north of Kailua to Highway 27 past Kawaihae. Turn left at the Mahukona sign and follow the road to the park. Across the bay from your entry place is an old shipwreck. A coral reef extends out to sea from the park. There's lots of old junk on the bottom of this bay. **Kapaa Beach Park** is a little farther up the road from Mahukona and is safe in the summer months only. Surf gets big here in the winter. If you're snorkeling, follow the shoreline. Water depth ranges between five and 15 feet near shore where you can explore rock ledges and small holes and crevices. Divers may want to cruise into deeper waters. The best way to plan this dive is to walk up the trail past the restrooms and enter off the rock ledge at the end of the trail. Then swim back toward the parking lot to the next cove. Be aware of currents, winds and large waves.

Captain Cook Discovers Kealekekua Bay

Captain James Cook set sail from Plymouth, England, in 1776 on his third expedition to the Pacific to map the then completely unknown Pacific Ocean and study it scientifically. These expeditions were the first of their kind. He spent two years crossing and exploring the South Pacific, stopping off at a number of south sea islands along the way. One of the expedition's goals was to find the northern limit of the Pacific. On January 18, 1778, sailing his flagship HMS Resolution with a second ship, HMS Discovery not far behind, Cook came upon Oahu. He didn't land there, however, sailing north to Kauai where he went ashore looking for provisions. The natives were very friendly and impressed with his ship. They soon developed a fascination for anything metallic, trading food and provi-

Diver with Lion fish. Photo courtesy of Cory Gray

Diving Hawaii

sions for scraps of iron. Cook and his men provisioned the boat, weighed anchor and turned their ships north to explore Alaskan waters.

A year later, Cook returned to the Hawaiian Islands from the coast of Alaska. Winter was approaching and he was looking for a safe anchorage. He surveyed Maui, but after completely mapping its shores, decided to continue on to the Big Island which he could see to the south. There at Kealakekua Harbor he dropped his anchor and went ashore.

What occurred was a series of events that were to spell disaster for Cook, the greatest navigator and explorer of his time. To the Hawaiians, the arrival of Captain Cook and his giant sailing vessels was the fulfillment of a legend. It was a time of celebration for the God Lono who, according to legend, was said to favor this particular harbor on the island above all others. The Hawaiians decided Cook was Lono and paid the appropriate homage to the returning god.

This celebration lasted for over a month. The Hawaiians generously and freely supplied Cook's boat with supplies and the crew with their women. But, unknown to Cook, this was a test (Hawaiian gods don't need women). During all the celebrating, seaman Watman, one of Cook's crew, died. He was buried at Hikiau Heiau where a plaque marks the event to this day. The Hawaiians began to suspect these gods might be impostors and relations became strained. So on February 4, 1779, Cook and his crew set sail, but bad weather forced them to turn back to Kealekekua Bay.

The Hawaiians, now totally hostile, greeted the ships by throwing rocks. They then stole a small boat which Cook's men retrieved but in doing so, roughed up an alii (holy man) as the natives watched in horror. The Hawaiians retaliated by stealing a small cutter from the Discovery which infuriated Cook. He went ashore with nine marines to take one of the chiefs hostage until the cutter was returned. This proved to be his fatal mistake. In the ensuing struggle, another lesser chief was killed which started a riot with the 20,000 Hawaiians present there. Cook's marines took to their boats and poised just a few feet offshore, motioned Cook to swim out to them. But, Cook, one of the most renown explorers and master navigators of all time, stood on the rocks in about a foot of water — he couldn't swim. A blow to the head and Cook went down and his body was hacked into piece by 20,000 very angry natives.

Kona Aggressor

If you're in the mood for a week or two of non-stop diving, you might consider a voyage aboard the live-aboard Kona Aggressor operating out of Kailua-Kona. This boat has everything from luxurious air-conditioned staterooms with private bath w/shower, full service galley, jacuzzi, photographic seminars, and certification classes.

For more information:

Kona Aggressor
Live/Dive Hawaii Inc.
P.O. Box 2097
Kailua-Kona, Hawaii 96745
(800) 344-KONA, (808) 329-2446

Emergency Numbers

Ambulance, Fire (808) 961-6022
Coast Guard (808) 935-6370, 889-6454
DAN (Divers Alert Network) (919) 684-8111

Weather Information (808) 961-5582

Hilo Hospital
1190 Waianuenue Ave
Hilo, HI 96720
(808) 969-4111

Kona Hospital
Kealakekua Town
Kono, HI 96750
(808) 322-9311

Hawaii Visitors Bureau
250 Keawe St.
Hilo, HI 96720
(808) 961-5797

Hawaii Visitors Bureau
75-5719 West Alii Dr.
Kailua – Kona, HI 96740
(808) 329-7787

Dive Shops & Boats

Name, Address, Phone	Reference#	Hour	Affiliation	Compressor	Rentals	Repairs	Comments
Big Island Divers 74-425 Kealakehe Pkwy #7 Kailua-Kona, HI 96740 (808) 329-6068	001	8am- 6pm Daily	PADI 5-Star	4000 psi	Y	Y	
Fair Wind 78-7128 Kaleopapa Rd. Keauhou Bay Kona, HI 96740 (808) 322-2788; (800) 872-4341	002	7:30am- 5pm Daily			Y		Snorkel gear Dives/Snorkel boat dives
Jack's Diving Locker Kono Inn Shopping Village & Coconut Grove Shopping Center 75-5819 Alii Dr. Kailua-Kona, HI 96740 (800) 345-4807 (808) 329-7585	003	8am-6pm Daily	NAUI PADI	3000 psi	Y	Y	
King Kamehameha Divers 75-5660 Palani Rd. Kailua-Kona, HI 96740 (800) 525-7234 (808) 329-5662	004	7am-7pm M-Sat 7am-5pm Sun	PADI 5-Star IDC	3000 psi	Y	Y	Two Tank Morning Charter
Kohala Divers Ltd. Kawaihae Shopping Center P.O. Box 4935 Kawaihae, HI 96743 (808) 882-7774	005	8am-5pm Daily	PADI	3500 psi	Y	Y	Full Service Dive Shop
Kona Coast Divers 75-5614 Palani Rd. Kailua-Kona, HI 96740 (800) 562-3483 (808) 329-8802	006	7am-6pm Daily	PADI NAUI SSI	4000 psi	Y	Y	
Nautilus Dive Center 382 Kamehameha Ave. Hilo, HI 96720 (808) 935-6939	006	9am-4pm M-Sa Closed Sun	PADI	3000 psi	Y	Y	
Ocean Splash King's Shops Shopping Center Waikoloa, HI 96743 Phone #????????????	007	7am-6pm Daily	PADI NAUI				
Ocean Sports Waikoloa Waikoloa Beach Resort P.O. Box 5000 HCO2 Kohala Coast, HI 96743 (808) 885-5555; (800) 835-8538	008	7am-6pm Daily	PADI NAUI				Boat Trips Twice a Day
Sandwich Isle Divers 76-5729 I Alii Drive Kailua-Kona, HI 96740 (808) 329-9188	009	8am-8pm Daily	PADI NAUI	3300 psi	Y	Y	
AAA Dive Kona P.O. Box 1780 Kailua-Kona, HI 96745 (800) 562-3483	A						Charter Boats Only
Aggressor Fleet Kona Aggressor P.O. Drawer K Morgan City, LA 70381 (800) 348-2628	B						Charter Boats Only
Aquatic Adventures P.O. Box 610 Moon's Crater Kamuela, HI 96743 (808) 885-6303	C						Charter Boats Only

Dive Shops & Boats

Name, Address, Phone	Reference#	Hours	Affiliation	Compressor	Rentals	Repairs	Comments
Dive Makai Charters P.O Box 2955 74-5590 Alapa St. Kailua-Kona, HI 96745 (808) 329-2025	D						Charter Boats Only
Dolphin Divers P.O. Box 4640 Kailua-Kona, HI 96745	E						Charter Boats Only
Fantasy Divers 73-4125 Hawaii Belt Rd. Kailua-Kona, HI 96740	F						Charter Boats Only
Gold Coast Divers 75-5744 Alii Dr. Kailua-Kona, HI 96740	G						Charter Boats Only
Kona Aggressor (Live-Dive Hawaii, Inc.) P.O. Box 2097 Kailua-Kona, HI 96745 (800) 344-5662 (808) 329-8182	H						Charter Boats Only
Kona Coast Divers 75-5641 Palani Rd. Kailua-Kona, HI 96741 (800) 562-3483, (808) 329-8802	I						Charter Boats Only
Kona Scuba Seafaris 76-6241 Alii Drive, #3 Kailua-Kona, HI 96740 (800) 657-7704, (808) 326-2311)	J						Charter Boats Only
Kona Reef Divers c/o Kona Village Resort P.O. Box 1409 Kamuela, HI 96743	K						Charter Boats Only
Mauna Lani Sea Adventures Mauna Lani Hotel P.O. Box 4000 Kawaihae, HI 96743 (808) 885-7883	L						Charter Boats Only
Mauna Loa Diving Service 97 Haili St. Hilo, HI 96720 (808) 935-3299	M						Charter Boats Only
Sea Dreams Hawaii 77-6470 Leilani St. Kailua-Kona, HI 96740 (800) 366-3483; (808) 329-8744	N						Private Lessons Only
A Sea Paradise, Scuba P.O. Box 5655 Kailua-Kona, HI 96745 (800) 322-5662; (808) 322-2500	O						Private Lessons Only
Sun Seeker P.O. Box 2442 Kailua-Kona, HI 96745 (808) 322-6774	P						Private Lessons Only
Volcano Island Dive P.O. Box 390847 Kailua-Kona, HI 96739 (808) 326-9311	Q						Charter Boats Only

DIVE SPOTS

	Dive Spot	Depth	Expertise	Boat or Beach
Three Room Cavern & Two Story Caves	(300)	40-55 feet	Advanced	Boat
Honaunau Bay	(301)	10-100 feet	Beginner to Advanced	Beach
Kealakekua Bay	(302)	10-30 feet	All levels	Beach
Red Hill	(303)	10-70 feet	Intermediate	Boat
Old Airport	(304)	15-120 feet	All levels	Boat
Kiawi Point	(305)	10-120 feet	All levels	Boat
Pine Trees	(306)	35-90 feet	All levels	Boat
Keahole Point	(307)	20-50 feet	All levels	Beach
Puako	(308)	10-90 feet	Intermediate	Beach
Pentagon	(309)	15-40 feet	All levels	Boat
Horseshoe Canyon	(310)	10-80 feet	Intermediate	Boat
Lapakahi State Historical Park	(311)	10-30 feet	All levels	Beach
Mahukona Beach Park	(312)	10-60 feet	All levels	Beach
Kapaa Beach Park	(313)	10-60 feet	All levels	Beach

Distance Chart Miles

Hilo-Kalapana 26
Hilo-Volcano House 31
Hilo-Kailua via Naalehul . . 25
Hilo-Kailua, via
   Saddle Road 87
Hilo-Kailua, via
   Hamakua 93
Kailua-Keahole Airport . . . 7

Photo courtesy of Rick Baker

Hawaii—The Big Island

Kilauea Crater. Photo by Warren Bolster, courtesy of the Hawaii Visitors Bureau

Clearly the best dive tours on Kauai...

KAUAI, THE OLDEST AND LUSHEST of the Hawaiian Islands, harbors an adundance of spectacular diving areas along its rich shores. Experience the ultimate beauty of coral encrusted reefs, lava tubes and brightly colored fish. All of this beauty exsists beneath the warm waters of Kauai. Let us take you there aboard the magnificent **RAINSONG**, a 70 foot masterpiece that will accommodate your every need. Our featured tours include full day and half-day excursions plus exclusive dive tours to the neighboring island of Niihau with its pristine seascapes and plentiful marine life.

COMPLETE DIVE PACKAGES... We can arrange for you a variety of custom dive packages including condominium or hotel, car rental, activities, & air fare. Special requests welcome. Call us **TOLL FREE** for current package and rental rates or diving information:

1-800-822-9422

AQUATICS KAUAI

Located at: 733 Kuhio Highway, Kapaa, Kauai, HI 96746 • (808) 822-9213

PACIFIC OCEAN

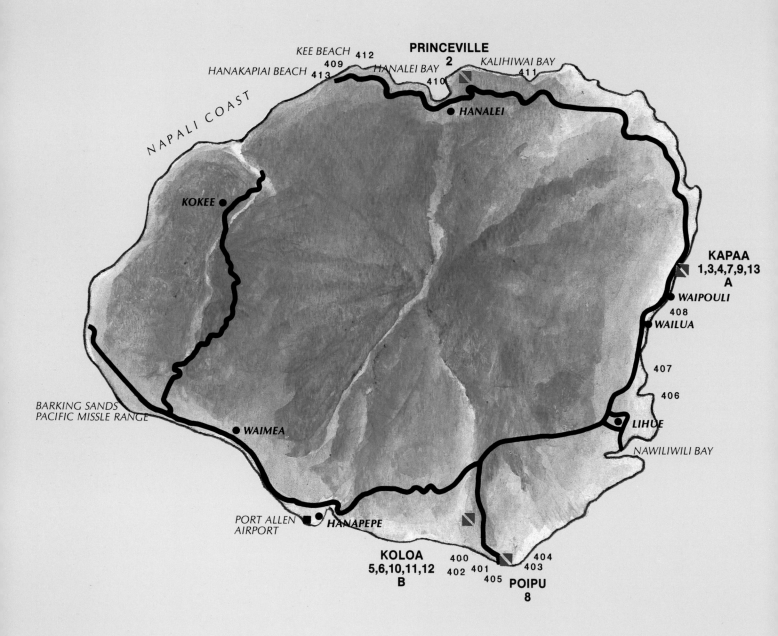

PACIFIC OCEAN

KEE BEACH 412
HANAKAPIAI BEACH 409
413

PRINCEVILLE
2

KALIHIWAI BAY
411

HANALEI BAY
410

● HANALEI

NAPALI COAST

● KOKEE

KAPAA
1,3,4,7,9,13
A

● WAIPOULI
408
● WAILUA

407

406

BARKING SANDS
PACIFIC MISSLE RANGE

● WAIMEA

LIHUE

NAWILIWILI BAY

PORT ALLEN
AIRPORT

● HANAPEPE

KOLOA
5,6,10,11,12
B

400
402   401
405

404
403

POIPU
8

N

THIS MAP IS NOT TO BE USED
FOR NAVIGATIONAL PURPOSES

KAUAI
The Garden Island
Including Niihau

Kauai is the only Hawaiian island that was formed from a single erupting volcano. This volcanic mountain-island, the northernmost in the chain, rests on the Pacific sea bottom 100 miles northwest of Honolulu. Because there is only one volcanic mountain, Mount Waialeale, the island has a circular shape. Waialeale stands 5,148 feet above sea level and is said to be the wettest place on earth with over 400 inches of rainfall a year. Over the centuries, this enormous level of rainfall has eroded the volcanic rock of the island, washing down the slopes of Waialeale, filling and flattening the now wide valley floors of Kauai. These fertile valleys that divide the numerous mountain ranges in the interior are so flat, wide and filled with a continuous flow of rainwater cascading from the peaks of Waialeale that Kauai can boast the only navigable river in the Hawaiian Islands. Boat rides up Wailua River offer a relaxing way to see part of the interior of Kauai and the famous Fern Grotto.

But don't let this report of high rainfall scare you away from visiting Kauai. Rainfall around the island's perimeter, especially along the eastern and southern coastline, is an inconsequential 5 inches a year. It is only at the very peak of Waialeale where the warm clouds that rise off the Pacific are cooled and condensed that you will find 400-plus inches of rain a year. Kauai is truly an island paradise.

But the waters from Waialeale have worked more magic on Kauai than just the river Wailua. The erosive power of the rain and the fact that Kauai is the oldest of the islands has left nature's signature all over the island. The rain has rounded the mountains, depositing rich volcanic soil from the mountaintops into the valleys below. Rivers have had time to cut deep and wide, producing many streams and beautiful waterfalls. Many streams and rivers flow down the slopes from Waialeale toward the ocean. Within these valleys an abundance of lavish volcanic soil has developed and supports a rich botanical diversity which is reflected in the numerous botanical gardens you can tour on the island. Some of the animal life here is found nowhere else in the world. Because of its lush countryside Kauai has earned the name "Garden Isle."

The vast amounts of flowing water have also formed a great gorge that cuts across the northern portion of the island called Waimea Canyon. Beautiful waterfalls and rainbows adorn this giant valley called the "Grand Canyon of the Pacific." You can get a spectacular view of this valley by just driving up Highway 550 on the way to Kokee State Park. On up the same road in the park you will find a vantage point where you can gaze upon the northwest shores of Kauai and the Na Pali coastline far below. Here, too, rainwater and the mighty Pacific ocean have worked together to form this magnificent coastline with cliffs towering 4,000 feet above the pounding Pacific surf.

Kauai also has a surplus of two other vacation essentials: peace and quiet. These are enhanced by beautiful, white sand beaches formed by clear, warm tropical water. This is one Pacific island where you can wave the white flag at the Mainland and settle in for some real rest and relaxation. The largest town, Kapaa, has fewer than 5,000 residents. The biggest settlement on the island, Lihue, is barely a town but hosts the one main airport. Resorts and hotels offer good dining and entertainment, but generally the nightlife is quiet.

The island has three resort areas: Poipu Beach on the south shore, the Coconut Coast on the eastern shore and Princeville on the north shore.

The newest resort is the Westin Kauai near Lihue. Condominiums, private homes and estates are all available for rental. You can also rent cottages or cabins in the high country in the mountains of Kokee State Park. There are close to 8,000 units available for rent by tourists on the island.

Following page: Wailua Falls, nature crowned in glory. Photo by Peter French, courtesy of Hawaii Visitors Bureau

Kauai—The Garden Island

Most people rent a car on Kauai, despite the fact that there are some very good tours available. Roads are in excellent shape, but don't totally circumnavigate the entire island. The main drag, the Prince Kuhio Highway, hugs the coastline and deadends on either side of the Na Pali Coast on the island's northwest side. This rugged range of hanging valleys and tall cliffs probably has the best hiking in all the islands.

The rounded shape of Kauai leaves the majority of its shoreline exposed to the high winds and surf of the North Pacific. When the winds are calm, some of the best beaches for snorkeling and scuba can be found along the northeast coast between Anahola and Kee. Some are protected by a fringing reef so if the weather is not cooperating for diving, excellent snorkeling and sun bathing is still possible. Along the southwestern coast some of the boat dives are divable even when the weather isn't totally cooperating.

When the wind and waves are calm the diving and snorkeling on Kauai is incredible. But if you land on the island at a bad time there is still some good news. Along these beautiful beaches, well kept campgrounds and parks are starting points for hiking trails that will take you into Kauai's interior. Here you can camp or just spend the day walking through a beautiful, tropical, Hawaiian dreamland.

In addition, Kauai has some excellent museums, botanical gardens and historical sites. It's hard to go wrong on the isle of Kauai.

Exploring Kauai

From the town of Lihue on Kauai's southwestern shore you can tour the island in two directions, north or south, both leading to a dead end at the Na Pali Coast State Park on the northwest shore on the opposite end of the island. The eastern route takes you to the end of the road at a vantage point high in the mountains where you can look down on the state park. The northern route also takes you to the end of the road at the edge of the beach where you can hike along this same beautiful coastline. Leave a whole day for each excursion. Both are experiences you won't soon forget.

The Eastern Route

In the town of Lihue you can get an overview of the island's history at the **Kauai Museum** on Rice Street. You'll learn about the island's geologic history and some of its social structure. Also on Rice Street is the **Hawaiian Visitor Bureau** and the U.S. Post Office. Not far from there on Nawiliwili Road in Lihue is the **Grove Farm Home-**

Erosion plays a major role in the topography of Kauai. Photo courtesy of Ron Owen

Kauai—The Garden Island

stead Museum which has been preserved exactly as it was when the last of the Wilcox family died. Relics from several historical eras are displayed in the house. You get the feeling that the last inhabitant of this old Hawaiian plantation just walked out the door one day and could be back at any moment. From the Grove Homestead head toward the beach, turn right on Waapa Road then onto Hulemalu Road to get to the **Menehune Fish Pond**. The Menehunes are a primitive tribe that are thought to have lived on the island before the Polynesians arrived. According to legend, they constructed the fish pond in one night between dusk and dawn. If you continue up the road and turn right on Puhi Road you'll get back to Highway 50. Turn left and head east.

A tunnel made of trees covers part of Highway 520 which you take off of Highway 50 to get to the town of Koloa. This is the site of the first sugar mill built on the island. Now converted into a shopping center, the **Koloa Sugar Mill** can be found at the end of Welileli Road. Nearby is the **St. Raphael Church** built in 1854, the oldest Catholic Church on the island. As you leave Koloa on Poipu Road, turn on Lawai Road and go to see the spectacular **Spouting Horn** where sea waves are forced into a lava tube and ejected dramatically skyward through an opening in the lava cliff.

Get back on Highway 50 and head north to Waimea. On the beach in town you can see the site where **Captain Cook** first landed on Kauai and nearby, before you pass the bridge into town, is the ruin of a **Russian fort** constructed by Russians in 1817.

From Waimea you can continue up the coast on Highway 50 to where the road ends, or travel north up the mountain on Highway 550. The road up the western coast is a little rough and ends at the Polihale State Park

and the Polihale Heiau. The park has restrooms and spectacular hiking along rugged cliffs that reach down to the surf. Nearby the ruin of the Polihale Heiau is said to be the place on the island where the souls of the dead come to enter oblivion.

About 10 miles up Highway 550 stop at the **Waimea Canyon Lookout** to get a spectacular view of the canyon below. A few more miles up the road is the **Kokee State Park** where you can take a hike on several nature trails. The road passes the Kokee Natural History Museum, the **Kokee Lodge** where you can rent a cabin, and the Park Headquarters where you can get information about the nature trails. The road ends at the **Puu o Kila Lookout** where you can get another spectacular view, this time of Kauai's north shore and an overall view of the Na Pali Coast State Park.

The Northern Route

Traveling north out of Lihue on Highway 56 the road takes you to

Waimea Canyon cuts across the northern portion of Kauai. Photo courtesy of Bill Shofstall

Kauai—The Garden Island

the town of Wailua. The Wailua River is the state's only navigable river. Up Highway 580 a little ways you can see **Kamokila**, a re-created ancient Hawaiian Village. Boat trips up the Wailua River take you to the famous Fern Grotto, a cave filled with a variety of ferns. There are also several archaeological sites of ancient Hawaiians along the river.

Getting back on Highway 56 heading north you'll come to the town of Kilauea. Take the main road through town to the **Kilauea Lighthouse**, a National Historic Landmark. Farther north on Highway 56, in Hanalei, you will come across the **Waioli Mission House** built in 1863, now a museum. Highway 56 becomes 560 and ends at **Haena State Park** at **Kee Beach**. Here you can take an 11 mile hike along a trail that hugs the Na Pali Coast and leads to the mouth of the **Kalalau Valley**.

Getting There

Currently there are no nonstop flights into Kauai from the mainland. Flights out of Kauai's Lihue Airport connect with all the other islands. Most travelers pass through Oahu's international airport in Honolulu and then take the 25 minute flight to Kauai. Between Hawaiian Air and Aloha Airlines there are dozens of flights daily between Kauai and the islands of Oahu, Maui and Hawaii.

Lihue Airport is located a few miles out of Lihue and has no public transportation to and from town. This means you must either rent a car or take a taxi to get to your hotel. The airport is small, but includes all the major car rental services, lockers, a restaurant and bar.

Airport Phone Number:
  (808) 246-1440

Staying There

Just about all of the available rooms on Kauai can be found in four major regions: Lihue (western shore), Poipu Beach (southern shore), Wailua/Kapaa (eastern shore), Princeville/Hanalea (north shore). Of the 6,000 rooms available, about a third of them are condominiums.

Most of the diving is out of the western and southern shores and yet

From the lookout in Kokee State Park you can see down to the Na Pali Coast State Park. Photo courtesy of Bill Shofstall

the north shore offers some excellent diving when the weather is co-operating. For the most part it's easy to get to wherever you want to dive no matter where you stay on the island.

For hearty souls, Kauai offers some of the best camping on the island and a number of places to rent tents, stoves or even an RV or small camper.

Hiking & Camping

Only a small portion of Kauai (maybe 10%) is accessible by car. This makes this island one of the prime backpacking and hiking spots in the Hawaiian Islands. The hiking trails are plentiful and well maintained. Maps provided by the Department of Natural Resources will describe most of the hiking trails through-

out the federal, state and county parks.

Most trails offer an added bonus of either a botanical garden, a swimming hole or a beautiful view. Some of the trails transport you back in time to the days of the early Hawai-ians through historical landmarks and ancient ruins. The trails vary in difficulty from a 20 minute trek to weeks in some of the most strenuous yet beautiful terrain in the world.

Up at Kokee State Park there are a number of easy trails, affording some spectacular views of cliffs, canyons and waterfalls. Get a trail map and additional information from the ranger's booth. The Kalalau Trail on the Na Pali Coast is the trail on the island. You begin your walk at the end of Highway 56 at Kee Lagoon, pick up a map at the trail head, sign in and walk 11 miles through a time tunnel to a paradise close to the days of old Hawaii. Day use permits are required past Hanakapiai which is about 2 miles in along the trail.

Kauai—The Garden Island

Camping permits are required.

To get your map of the island's trails around the island contact:

Department of Natural Resources
Box 1671
Lihue, Kauai, HI 96766

One of the best islands in the Hawaiian Islands to camp or hike, Kauai offers a wide variety of camping to fit just about everyone's needs. You can backpack into one of the remote areas of the island and camp or drive up to your campsite and plug in your coffee maker. RV camping is permitted in many of the parks and RVs are available for rental. From the end of Highway 56 at Kee Beach hikers can take the Kalalau Trail to one of the most enchanted valleys in the Pacific or you can double back on the same highway and at Kohee State Park hike along trails and look down on the same cliffs of the Na Pali coast.

Except for Kokee State Park, the campgrounds of Kauai are built along the coastline. From the coast the hiking trails lead into the remote interior of the island. There are more than a dozen state and county parks that offer camping and up on the mountain Kokee State Park offers cabins. Permits are required at both county and state parks.

For camping rentals:

Beach Boy Campers
Box 3208
Luhue, HI 96766
(808) 245-9211

Hanalei Camping and Backpacking
Ching Young Village
Box 1245
Hanalei, HI 96714
(808) 826-6664

STATE PARKLANDS

Division of State Parks, Kauai District
P.O. Box 1671
3060 Eiwa St.
Lihue, HI 96766

(808) 245-4444
Ahukini State Recreational Pier. East of Lihue about 2 miles.

Haena State Park
North of Lihue off Highway 56, 40 miles. Hiking.

Kokee State Park
North of Kekeha off Highway 550. Tent and trailer camping, hiking, nature study, cabins, visitor center, restrooms.

Na Pali Coast State Park
North of Lihue off Highway 56. Remote, hiking, backpacking, tent camping.

Polihale State Park
North of Mana off Highway 50. Tent and trailer camping, showers, restrooms.

Russian Fort Elizabeth State Historical Park
Near Waimea off Highway 50. Historical Russian Fort, restrooms.

Wailua River State Park
North of Lihue off Highway 56. Riverboat cruise, beautiful Hawaiian river valley, sunbathing and safe swimming.

The lighthouse at Kilauea Point is no longer in use. Photo courtesy of Ronald Owen

Waimea Canyon State Park
North of Kekaha off Highway 550. Hiking.

COUNTY PARKLANDS

Kauai County Division of Parks and Recreation
4280 A Rice St. Bldg. B
Lihue, HI 96766
(808) 245-8821
Permit required for camping.

Anahola Beach Park
North of Lihue off Highway 56. Swimming, showers, restrooms.

Anini Beach Park
North of Lihue off Highway 56. Tent camping, swimming, showers, restrooms.

Haena Beach Park
North of Lihue off Highway 56. Tent and trailer camping, showers, restrooms.

Hanalei Beach Park
North of Lihue off Highway 56. Restrooms.

Hanalei Pavilion Park
North of Lihue off Highway 56. Showers, restrooms.

Hanamaulu Beach Park
North of Lihue off Highway 56. Tent and trailer parking, showers, restrooms.

Hanapepe Pavilion Park
South of Lihue off Highway 50. Restrooms.

Kapaa Beach Park
North of Lihue off Highway 56 Showers, restrooms.

Kekaha Beach Park
West of Lihue off Highway 50. Restrooms.

Lucy Wright Park
West of Lihue off Highway 50. Tent camping, showers, restroom.

Niumalu Beach Park
South of Lihue, end of Highway 58. Tent/trailer camping, showers, restrooms.

Kauai—The Garden Island

Poipu Beach Park
South of Lihue off Highway 50.
Showers, restrooms.

Salt Pond Park
South of Lihue, end of Highway 543.
Tent camping, showers, restrooms.

FEDERAL PARKLANDS
Hanalea National Wildlife Refuge
c/o P.O. Box 87
Kilauea, HI 96754
(808) 541-1201
Near Hanalea. Observations can be made
along Ohiki Rd by vehicle. Need special permit to enter park.

Huleia National Wildlife Refuge
c/o P.O. Box 87
Kilauea, HI 96754
(808)   541-1201
Special permit required; contact refuge manager.

**Kilauea Point National Wildlife
   Refuge**
c/o P.O. Box 87
Kilauea, HI 96754
(808) 541-1201
Near Kilauea. Parking, restrooms and
hiking.

Emergency Numbers

Ambulance, Fire 911
Coast Guard (800) 331-6176
DAN (Divers Alert Network) (919) 684-8111

Hyperbaric Chamber
Kauai Veteran's Memorial Hospital
4643 Waimea Canyon Dr.
Waimea, Kauai, HI
(808) 338-9431

Wilcox Memorial Hospital
3420 Kuhio Highway
Lihue, Kauai, HI 96766
(808) 245-1100

Mileage ChartMiles

Lihue-Haena   38
Lihue-Poipu   12
Lihue-Mana   33
END-5662
(808) 322-2500

*A National Wildlife Refuge exists at
Kilauea Point on the north shore of
Kauai. Photo courtesy of Bill Shofstall*

Diving Kauai

The majority of the dive operations on Kauai operate on the protected southern shore in Wailua, Koloa and Poipu. There is one dive operation with a boat on the northern shore out of Hanalei. Because of the shape of the island, many of its shores are subject to heavy surf and bad weather. Also, the large rivers dump volcanic silt along the coastline limiting much beach diving.

On Kauai, diving is only possible during the best weather conditions. Contact one of the many dive shops on the island to get help with where and when you should dive. Some offer guided beach dives. In the winter months all diving is restricted to the protected southern shore where dive boats transport divers to the dive site most of the year. Many of the best dives along the southern shore are boat dives. On the north shore, in the calm of Kauai's summer, you can venture out of Hanalei Harbor to dive some of the most pristine and unique dive spots in all the Hawaiian Islands. The north shore after the surf has died down (usually in the summer) offers some of the best beach diving on the island. The water is colder so expect to see more large fish and fewer corals.

When the waters are calm, some of the dive boat operations also take divers to the island of Niihau (the Forbidden Island) and to a small islet of the island's coast called Lehua. The island is privately owned and inhabited with a resident population of native Hawaiians. Visitors are not welcome on the island un-

Silhouette of diver over black coral. Photo courtesy of David McCray

less they are personally invited but the dive spots around Niihau are accessible by boat from Kauai. The trip takes about three hours, but the dive spots are pristine and the underwater features are spectacular.

Dive Spots

If you dive along the southern shore you will probably make boat dives at a number of dive spots. One popular dive is at the **General Store**. This dive spot got its name from the fact that you can find such a wide variety of underwater curiosities here. Large schools of lemon butterflyfish hover over this U-shaped rock formation that rises 40 feet from the sea bottom at 100 feet. Hammerhead, green sea turtles and manta rays have been spotted here. The store's inventory doesn't stop here, however. Add to the stock an old steamship scattered across the bottom plus numerous lava tubes and caves.

Nearby **Fishbowl** gets its name from the large schools of bluestriped snapper and other schooling fish that overwhelm divers. The depth of the dive ranges between 45-80 feet. **Turtle Hill** is home to a very large number of green sea turtles, as well as pennantfish, lobsters, and eels. Large flat rocks begin at 45 feet then drop off to about 95 feet. There are numerous arches, caves and ledges. Octopus, eagle rays and whitetip reef sharks are fairly common. **Sheraton Caves** is another one of those Hawaiian dive spots where the sea life has made a name for itself. Two sea turtles, Pepe and LaPue, show up at most of the dive boats to "work the crowd." If you are a photographer still trying to get that perfect turtle

shot, these guys are very professional. Other sea life includes eels and lots of schooling fish. Several miles long, **Brennecke's Ledge** is a flat shelf that drops off abruptly at about 50 feet to a depth of 90 feet. As you drop down over the edge of the drop-off you encounter many ledges and overhangs where you'll find longnose hawkfish hiding in branches of black coral trees. Schools of bluestriped snapper hover above. Whitetip reef shark, turtles and octopus are common.

Koloa Landing is mainly for beginners. This is one of the beaches where instructors bring their Scuba classes for their checkout dive. But if this is your first dive in a while and you're not feeling one hundred percent comfortable in the water, make this your first dive. The deepest you can get is 25 feet and a boat ramp makes for easy entry and exit. To get there drive south of Koloa on Poipu Road, then turn right where you see a Y in the road just past the shopping center. Turn left on Hoonani Road and before the 5 mile marker, turn right and drive down to the landing. Once in the water swim along the wall either to the right or left.

When the trade winds are not blowing along the eastern shore of Kauai there are a number of good boat dives. One is on the wreck of the **Andrea F. Luckenbach**, a 435 foot freighter sunk in 1951. Today she is scattered across a large area that starts about 300 yards offshore. At the **Aquarium**, named for its multitude of fish that overwhelms divers, your depth will range between 30 to 45 feet. At **Santa Claus Cave** you'll enter a lava tube whose en-

Diving Kauai

trance looks like a large fireplace. The tube drops down about 40 feet to an opening at the bottom.

On the north shore you have to get lucky and land in Kauai when the sea and wind are calm — usually in the summer months. This actually has a positive side because when you do dive here it has an untouched quality you don't find elsewhere in the islands. There is also the chance of seeing a fish that is very rare. **At Blue Bluffs** a vertical wall drops to about 100 feet. You'll find turtles, octopus and black coral trees. The **Oceanarium** is a group of pinnacles that start at about 75 feet and drop off to 120 feet or more. There are loads of fish hovering in the waters over the drop-off. Giant trees of black coral can be seen here too. At the **Truckstop** a giant archway dominates the dive spot. The sea bottom is in about 100 feet of water with cup coral of all colors covering the bottom.

Shore dives on the north shore are subject to weather and surf conditions. Once again, if you land on Kauai on that perfect day in the summer you will get access to an underwater world seldom seen. **Haena Point** is called "tunnels" by surfers to describe the type of waves that break in this area. To get there, get on Highway 56 to the north past Hanalei and past Wainiha until you see the 36.6 marker. Turn right on the dirt road and park at the end. Head straight out into the water. At about 35 feet you'll come across the drop-off. Cruise along the wall; to the left you'll find the bottom drops to about 60 feet. Small caves and ledges hide rudderfish, wrasses and a large, docile whitetip reef shark named "Big Mama." At the end of Highway 56 past Haena State Park is **Kee Beach**. Because of the fringing reef this is a great place for snorkeling in 10 to 20 feet of water. The beach is beautiful and you can take a hike on the Na Pali Coast hiking trail. If you want to put on a tank and if the water is calm, head outside of the reef where the depth drops to about 30 feet. You will find lots of caves and rock ledges to explore.

Again in the summer months, when the sea is calm, several of the dive operators will take you to the Forbidden Island of **Niihau** and to nearby **Lehua Rock**. The boat ride takes three hours to travel the 17 miles across the channel. If everything goes well with the weather you will dive in seemingly untouched Hawaiian underwater terrain. It is truly virgin Hawaiian diving and you are likely to see sharks, rays and other large marine life off the many drop-offs, canyons or under an archway.

Diver on Mahi, a wreck off the leeward side of Oahu. Photo courtesy of Cory Gray

Legend of the Menehune

Kauai is the only Hawaiian Island with a legend and supporting archaeological evidence of a civilization that may have lived here before the Polynesians arrived. The legend speaks of small aborigines called the Menehune. Stories told of these little people at times seem to parallel those stories told of leprechauns in Ireland, but there is scientific evidence. In the Kauai Museum in Lihue archaeological evidence and legend blend together convincing you that these little people did exist.

These were people who were hard workers and master stonemasons and are said to have built the fish pond in Niumalu in just one night. There are other mysterious landmarks around the island like the Menehune Ditch just out of Waimea on Highway 550. These people were also known to be practical jokers who loved to play games. According to historical Hawaiian accounts, the island's chief thought there was far too much intermarriage occurring between the Memehune and his people so he set them adrift on a raft and they were never seen again.

Theories of the origins of these people abound. Some historical experts think this was an entirely different race of people predating the Polynesians' arrival on the islands. Others feel this may have been a faction of the original Polynesian who, separated from tribes on the other islands, evolved separately into smaller people. Kauai is thought to be the first island the Polynesians landed on in about 200 A.D., some 500 years before the other islands were explored and settled.

Dive Shops & Boats

Name, Address, Phone	Reference#	Hour	Affiliation	Compressor	Rentals	Repairs	Comments
Aquatics Kauai 733 Kuhio Hwy Coconut Cove Shopping Center Kapaa, Kauai, HI 96746 (808) 822-9213 (800) 822-9422	001	8:30am-5:30pm Daily	PADI NAUI SSI	3000 psi	Y	Y	
Beach Activities of Kauai Sheraton Princeville Hotel P.O. Box 3250 Princeville, Kauai, HI 96722 (808) 826-6851	002	8am-7pm Daily	PADI	3000 psi	Y	Y	Trips to Niihau!
Bubbles Below 6251 Hauaala Rd. Kapaa, Kauai, HI 96746 (808) 822-3483	003	8am-5pm Daily					Two-tank boat dive - Trips to Niihau
Dive Kauai 976 Kuhio Highway Kapaa, Kauai, HI 96746 (808) 822-0452 (800) 828-3483	004	8am-5:30pm M-Sat 9am-3pm Sun	PADI 5-Star IDC Facility	3000 psi	Y	Y	
Fathom Five Divers P.O. Box 907 Poipu Rd (Next to Chevron Station) Koloa, Kauai, HI 96756 (808) 742-6991	005	7:30am-7:30pm M-Sat 7:30-4:30 Sun	PADI 5-Star	3000 psi	Y	Y	Full service dive shop.
Kauai Divers 3240 Poipu Rd Koloa, Kauai, HI 96746 (808) 742-7959	006	8am-6pm Daily	NAUI SSI PADI	3200 psi	Y	Y	Full service dive shop
Ocean Odyssey At Kauai Hilton & Beach Villas P.O. Box 957 Kapaa, Kauai, HI 96765 (808) 245-8681 (808) 742-6731	007	8:30am-5pm Daily	PADI		Y	Y	Boat dives seven days a week.
The Poipu Dive Company Kiahuna Shopping Village Poipu, Kauai, HI 96756 (808) 742-7661 (808) 742-1734	008	8am-9pm M-Sat 8am-6pm Sun	PADI	3000 psi	Y	Y	
Sea Sage Diving Center 4-1378 Kuhio Highway Kapaa, Kauai, HI 96746 (808) 822-3841	009	8am-5pm Daily	PADI NAUI SSI NASDS	3000 psi	Y	Y	
Sea Sports, Kauai 2827 Poipu Rd. Koloa, Kauai, HI 96756 (808) 742-9303	010	8am-6pm Daily	PADI NAUI		Y	Y	
Sea Sports, Kauai Sheraton Kauai Hotel P.O. Box 638 Koloa, Kauai, HI 96756 (808) 742-1221	011	8am-6pm Daily	PADI NAUI		Y	Y	
Sea Sports, Kauai Waiohai Beach Service c/o Stoffer Waiohai Hotel Koloa, Kauai, HI 96756 (808) 742-7051	012	8am-6pm Daily	PADI NAUI		Y	Y	

Dive Shops & Boats

Name, Address, Phone	Reference#	Hour	Affiliation	Compressor	Rentals	Repairs	Comments
Wet-N-Wonderful Ocean Sports P.O. Box 910 Kapaa, Kauai, HI 96746 (808) 822-0211	013	Open Daily	NAUI SSI PADI				Shore, boat and Scuba Training.
Get Wet Kauai 4442 Makaha Rd. Kapaa, Kauai, HI 96746 (808) 822-4884	A						Charter Boats Only
Waiohai Beach Service c/o Stoffer Waiohai Hotel Koloa, Kauai, HI 96756 (808) 742-7051	B						Charter Boats Only

DIVE SPOTS

	Dive Spot	Depth	Expertise	Boat or Beach
General Store	(400)	55-95 feet	Intermediate Advanced	Boat
Fishbowl	(401)	45-80 feet	Intermediate	Boat
Turtle Hill	(402)	45-95 feet	All levels	Boat
Sheraton Caves	(403)	30-70 feet	All levels	Boat
Brennecke's Ledge	(404)	50-90 feet	Intermediate Advanced	Boat
Koloa Landing	(405)	10-25 feet	All levels	Beach
Andrea F. Luckenbach	(406)	10-65 feet	All levels	Beach
Aquarium	(407)	30-45 feet	All levels	Boat
Santa Claus Cave	(408)	40 feet	Intermediate Advanced	Boat
Blue Bluffs	(409)	50-100 feet	Advanced	Boat
Oceanarium	(410)	65-120 feet	Advanced	Boat
Truckstop	(411)	50-100 feet	Intermediate	Boat
Haena Point	(412)	15-60 feet	All levels	Beach
Kee Beach	(413)	10-30 feet	All levels	Beach
Niihau	(414)	120 feet	Advanced	Boat

Following Page: Wreck of the Mahi of Oahu. Photo courtesy of Rick Baker

PART V

Instruction
&
Dive Data

Dive Data

Diving That Wreck

You're skimming over the bottom at 60 feet, turning the corner of a rocky outcropping, when suddenly you notice something unusual jutting up from the ocean floor. A little digging reveals a bit of brass, and you begin searching the area. Your adrenaline pumps as you anticipate the realization of the diver's foremost fantasy: finding an undiscovered wreck. Whether you dive for the sheer pleasure of underwater tranquility, to capture underwater life with camera, speargun or hand, every diver, at some time or another, has dreamed of finding the treasure of a sunken ship that plied the waters centuries ago.

In the warm waters that surround the islands you will find scores of wrecks, some sunk intentionally for sport divers; some not. In some areas ancient Hawaiian artifacts can be found. In many areas these wrecks and artifacts are protected. Find out the facts before you remove anything from the sea floor.

Many of the known wrecks have been altered so as to be relatively safe to dive by the casual, vacationing scuba diver. Large portions of the hull have been cut away so that access to the surface is but a few kicks away. Any sharp or hazardous area has been shored up, sharp points cut away. Off a dive boat with a guide these dives can be safe and extremely enjoyable.

If you're diving an unknown wreck, wreck diving can be dangerous. Rusting metal hulks and disintegrating wooden galleons are constantly decomposing beneath the water, and the mere presence of a diver may accelerate the process.

The unwary diver might just meet the fate of the ship's crew. The first rule of wreck diving is obvious: never go alone. Diving a known wreck offers the advantage of careful preparation. Take extra tanks; experienced wreck divers use two sets of doubles and a pony tank. It allows you more time to explore and provides a back-up system in case of trouble. Also, when the excitement of a good find has you using air more rapidly, or pushing your bottom time to the limit, the extra air can be a lifesaver. A dive computer and decompression line are essential since wreck diving necessarily involves a lot of bottom time. Buddy divers should each have a computer and compare readings using the more conservative meter in the case of any discrepancy. A light is also a necessity, both for exploring and keeping in touch with your partner. Many wrecks have dark holes and overhangs that can't be explored safely without a light, and it will be helpful in investigating points of interest. A knife is also essential, and a second knife is advised. Entanglements on wrecks are more common than not. A calm, well-prepared approach will keep them from getting you in serious trouble. Finally, carry a spool of line to mark your exit should you decide to explore inside the ship's carcass.

Many experienced wreck divers carry a tool kit, both for safety and to help them explore. Lines with floats for making objects you wish to return to, hammers, and an adjustable wrench, and a small file are among the items in these kits.

If you have cleared this wreck with the authorities and you want to take something to the surface, you'll have additional needs. If it's small and you can carry it, all well and good. Heavier, bulkier items need lift bags. Attached to your find, end-down, the bag is given air from a separate tank (using your mouthpiece can be dangerous) and the bag lifts the item to the surface.

Stay clear of your find if accompanying it to the surface with lift bags, and don't put more air in the bag than necessary to get it moving toward the surface, as it will accelerate as it goes up.

Remember, the first question for wreck divers is, "Who owns the find?" A good rule of thumb is to figure the more valuable the find, the more touchy the legalities. If you're lucky enough to discover an unknown wreck, you'll have to stake your claim and do some research to learn who has jurisdiction, what claims exist, and what your rewards might be. All of that becomes easier, however, if you decide to take on the challenge of a known wreck that has never before been subjected to salvage.

Pre-salvage contracts are the best approach in this case. Once you discover the joy of wreck diving, it can be addictive. Whether your first find is a small brass plate from a recent wreck or the ship's bell from a centuries-old galleon, the thrill of finding and recovering the legacy of the sea is something you'll want to repeat.

Wreck Dive Safety

A. All basic safety rules applying to ordinary sport diving should be followed, including the buddy system. You and your partner should be familiar with each other and rehearse emergency ascents and other vital procedures in advance.

B. Remember to ascend with a good supply of air remaining, keeping in mind that more active diving necessitates more air. Bottom time should be adjusted accordingly to compensate for increased air usage.

C. Be cautious when entering a wreck, checking for stability and making certain it will not cave in. Examine the structure as you would check handholds for security when mountain climbing. Special caution is called for when exploring rotting timber shipwrecks. Include in your equipment two reliable lights and a return line to guide you out of the wreck should your lighting fail.

D. When diving a wreck, don't attempt to carry more than you are able to carry comfortably. Be certain your flotation device can easily support your "treasures." Remember that you are endangering those divers below you if your load is not secure in your ascent. The usual procedure in wreck diving is to gather all items into one area and then take them up in your "lift" sack.

Boat Diving

No Hawaiian dive vacation would be complete without at least one boat dive. Some of the best dive sites are accessible only off of a dive boat. Look in the Dive Boat Section, under the individual island, to find a dive shop with a dive boat listing. Stop by the shop or call them. Ask a lot of questions before you're on the boat on your way out to the dive spot. Where is the boat going? Some of these operations go to specific spots on certain days of the week. What skill level will the divers on the boat be

No Hawaiian vacation would be complete without at least one boat dive. Photo courtesy of Rick Baker

diving at or how difficult are the dive spots where the boat is going? Hawaiian waters are famous for their sudden shifts in wind and their strong currents so ask about the weather and the dive conditions for that week. If you want to hunt, find out if that is possible. Many dive locations are marine reserves. Ask how many people will be on the boat (You may want a smaller charter). Finally, find out what time you should show up in the morning.

Usually you can do all your paperwork at the dive store the day before the dive. Rent any gear you might need, show your C-card and pay your money. Most boats have two tanks and weights already on the boat which are included with the charter. So either bring your own regulator, BC, gloves, mask, fins and snorkel or expect to rent them at the shop. Water temperatures average about 78 degrees, which can chill you after a short time in the water. You may want to

bring or rent a shortie or bring one from home.

A reputable boat will have a boat dive master or, on a smaller craft, require someone in your group to serve in that capacity. The boat dive master should be a Certified Advanced Diver, preferably the most experienced aboard. He should not participate in the dive and should only enter the water if necessitated by an emergency. His job is to coordinate the dive, both with the divers and with the skipper and crew of the vessel, to see to the safety of the divers, and to keep things going smoothly so that the diving is safe and everyone has a good time. The dive master should be completely familiar with the dive site and brief the divers before entering the water. He will draw up the teams, keep the logs, brief you on each dive, check certification, licenses and oversee legal matter such as waivers and catch limits.

There are certain courtesies and rules of etiquette to boat diving that you should observe to make it a pleasant experience for all involved.

Be prepared and be on time. Once out of the harbor you may find yourself paying for a dive trip and unable to dive due to your own forgetfulness. Most of the boats keep some spare equipment on board just in case someone forgets a mask or a regulator, but don't count on it. Use a checklist to make sure you have all your equipment, that your tank is full (if not provided), and that your gear is all in order. Be sure to carry your certification card and a current fishing license if you plan to take game. And don't forget money to pay for the charter, to cover refilling your tank and galley fees if these things are not included in the price. Most charter trips in the islands include snacks, drinks and lunch if you're going to be out for any length of time. If you brought your own equipment, make sure it is marked. This not only helps you, the other divers and the crew to prevent mix-ups, but it can be an aid in identifying you in the water.

Plan to arrive at least a half-hour before departure, and if you haven't done so already, sign the boat roster as soon as you get on board. Then check in with the dive master and follow his instructions or those of a designated crew member in stowing your gear. Most dive boats have racks for tanks and weight belts. Use them. If tanks are already on board, get assigned to a tank and set up your gear. Attach the regulator and BC to the tank so you are all ready to go when you get to the dive spot. Get your weight belt together and set it next to your tank. A classic no-no is to not fasten your tank securely or leave it unattended on the deck upright and have it roll over on someone's foot. This is second only to the problem of people stacking their gear in a convenient corner. Stowing your gear in an organized manner at the designated place not only helps you keep better track of it, but keeps it from interfering with others' enjoyment. If carrying a speargun, remember that loaded spearguns are not allowed on or near a boat, and tips should be covered to prevent accidental injury to yourself or others.

En route to the dive site you'll have a chance to get to know your fellow divers, the ship and the crew. You should also get a briefing from the dive master or skipper on the dive site and prevailing conditions. On many of the boats the dive master will talk to all the divers and ascertain the skill level of each diver. This will help him make the decision as to where you will be diving. Many dive boats will require you to sign a waiver, a legal document that should be treated seriously. If you've deter-

mined that you have chartered an acceptable craft with trained personnel, the waiver should cause you no reservations. It is your statement that you are aware of the risks of diving and will not hold the charter operators liable for anything that goes wrong that is not caused by their negligence.

At the dive site, use caution when suiting up. Naturally, everyone is anxious to get in the water, but by using a buddy system to suit up and by being aware of others on deck with you, you can avoid embarrassing entanglements that could delay the dive. The buddy system is also recommended for checking your gear to be sure everything is in order, and a conscientious dive master will make a final check before you enter the water. Don't walk around the boat with your fins on: they should be put on just before you enter the water. Enter the water only when given the OK by the dive master or designated crew member.

Entering the water can be accomplished safely in a couple of ways. In most cases the boat will have a swim step you can sit on and use to slide yourself into the water. A second method of entry is the "giant stride" method generally used when entering the water from an opening on either side of the boat. Bent slightly forward at the waist, the diver takes a large step off the side of the boat into the water while holding the face mask with one hand and weight belt with the other. If the boat is smaller you may want to just sit on the gunwale and roll into the water. Facing the center of the boat with both feet inside, extend as much of your body as possible over the water while leaning forward to counterbalance. Place one hand on your mask and the other on your weight belt buckle. When you're ready, just sit up, lean backward and let the weight of the

diving equipment carry you over the side. Camera gear or spear guns should be handed to you by a crew member after you have entered the water.

As a general rule, a diver should always enter the water slowly, using the method that will result in the least physical discomfort and disturbance to equipment. Each diver should determine the method best suited to various water conditions. Once in the water, give the dive master the OK signal and then swim at least 20 feet from the craft before adjusting your equipment so the next diver can enter the water.

Be sure you are familiar with signals that will be used between divers and the boat and particularly the boat's underwater recall system. Common signals are a raised right arm to signal pick up, and any erratic movements indicate you have a problem.

On most boats a guide will dive with the whole group taking them on a tour of the dive spot. If you are not familiar with the dive spot this can greatly enhance your dive. These guides know where every octopus or eel lives and usually will lead you through a lava tube or a cave you may not have been able to find yourself.

If you are new to boat diving, be sure to let the dive master know. Don't be embarrassed; everyone has a first time. It will alert him and the crew to watch for the problems that first-time boat divers can experience. For one thing, from shore you can gradually condition yourself to the depth; from a boat you are committed with no pre-conditioning once you jump. Relax, accustom yourself to your

Scuba dive over a rocky reef teaming with life in the morning, have a picnic lunch and hike up into the lush Hawaiian jungle in the afternoon. Photo courtesy of Rick Baker

surroundings and make sure you're over the dive site described in the briefing. Vertigo can also be a problem if you have lost association with the surface and have not yet reached bottom. Use your depth gauge to make sure you're descending and watch the bubbles from your regulator to make sure they are vertical. Finally, if you're doing a drift dive in a current, don't struggle against the current if you become disoriented. Remember your briefing and surface if you can't get your bearings. Find the boat and signal for a pick up.

When exiting the water into a boat, there are two general rules to remember and follow. First, exiting begins while the diver is still submerged. While ascending, the diver should continually look up and around to ensure that the boat is not directly overhead and that he will not strike it when surfacing. Holding an arm over the head is a good practice. Exhaling on ascent will give a clear indication to the surface that a diver is ascending. After surfacing the crew member will probably tell you to remove your tank and maybe your weight belt in the water. Remember to put a little air in your BC if you haven't already done so. Once the crew member has removed and stowed your tank, climb up on the swim step and remove your fins. Hand them to a crew member and then stand and step onto the boat.

If you're on a drift dive you will want to surface and signal the boat to pick you up. Divers are not usually picked up on a first-up system, but rather according to the current, with the most down-current diver being first. When waiting to be picked up, stay back from the craft and don't get under the diver getting on the swim step ahead of you. A dropped weight belt can be quite hazardous if it hits you.

Once back in the boat, stow your gear in the designated place and put any game or souvenirs where you are told. Don't embarrass yourself or the crew by trying to bring aboard illegal game. Clean your fish only in a designated place and never throw waste overboard while the other divers are still in the water.

Common sense dictates that no alcoholic beverages should be consumed prior to diving, and bringing illegal drugs of any kind on board puts you, the vessel and your fellow passengers in jeopardy.

Move in a slow and relaxed manner. Photo courtesy of Rick Baker

After the dive you can relax, have a snack and enjoy the ride home. You'll find the scenery to and from the dive site almost as good as the diving itself.

Beach Diving

If you take some precautions, beach diving along the beautiful shores of the Hawaiian Islands can really add dimension to your holiday. Many of the beach dives are in state parks, some in remote areas. These areas provide easy access to dive sites where you can scuba over a rocky reef teaming with fish in the morning, have a picnic lunch and then hike up into the lush Hawaiian jungle in the afternoon. On most of the islands high surf is a possibility no matter which shore you dive. A good rule of thumb is to expect the highest surf on the north shore of each island. If the surf is too high, don't dive. Consult with a local dive shop to get weather and surf information. Stay informed. If the surf looks reasonable, then go for it!

When you first get to the beach, take time and watch the surf. As waves enter the surf zone they touch bottom, rise and fall over themselves breaking on the shore line. Determine the height of the waves. Try to figure out how many waves to a set. This will give you an idea of when the smaller waves will be coming in. A wave set is a group of perhaps 10 waves where the last three are the largest. After the big ones hit the pattern starts over with a series of small waves. Try to time it so to enter and exit when the small waves are breaking, right after the big ones have just come in. Also, look for rip currents or for the presence of a strong longshore current. Be familiar with the tides, currents and conditions in the area. Again, it never hurts to ask for information at the local dive store.

Remember to plan your dive and dive your plan. Decide where and how you will enter and exit the water ahead of time. If there is a current decide to swim into the current for the first part of the dive so you can relax when you are tired on the way back.

When you are ready to dive, get your gear on. Walk with your buddy to the water's edge and put on your fins and mask. Place one hand on your mask, put your regulator in your mouth, and back slowly into the water. Some more experienced divers may opt to enter without fins and don them in the water past the surf zone. With this method you do run the risk of losing a fin or not having the kicking power if you need it to get out past the surf but you do gain some stability in larger surf. Always watch the waves both when entering and exiting the water. One of the biggest mistake divers make at this point is not keeping a constant eye on the incoming waves. Waves are unrelenting; they can and will surprise you. When you think you are deep enough to get under the waves, drop down and start swimming out past the wave zone. If the waves are large you may need to hold on to a rock on the bottom or dig your knife into the sand while the wave passes overhead. As the wave passes, kick a little to keep from being pulled back. Once the wave passes you will find the back wash will help you kick out into the deeper water.

Out past the surf zone pump a little air into your BC, relax, get together with your buddy. Check each other's equipment, go over your dive plan. Then begin your dive.

When it comes time to get out of the water, hang offshore and evaluate conditions. Figure out the

Rocky beach on the Big Island of Hawaii. Photo courtesy of Rick Baker

best way to get out of the water. Conditions may have changed during your dive so you may want to get out somewhere else. With regulator in mouth, BC deflated (too much buoyancy and the wave will grab you and toss you onto the beach) follow the smallest waves back into the beach. Swim until you can stand up in a couple feet of water. The farther in the better.

If the water is calm, choose the dignified exit standing and backing out, fins on, up the beach face. Again, always keep your eyes on the incoming waves. Walk well past the zone of wet sand before you take your fins and mask off. If the surf is a little large and the back wash feels strong, crawl up the beach face on all fours. This keeps your center of gravity low and makes it impossible to be knocked down when you're on your hands and knees.

Keeping these few rules in mind can help guarantee a fun and exciting trouble-free dive. Remember, if there is any doubt in

into day as you suit up with your dive buddies on a quiet beach on Maui. The gentle, warm tropical breeze rustles the broad leaves of the palm trees nearby and seems to intensify the excitement you feel in your gut. Backing into the dark waters you turn and push out into the warm water. Face down in the water you turn on your light, shining it down toward the bottom. The explosion of color is overwhelming as this

In the darkened environment your entire focus is on the one beam of light in front of you. You become more aware of the warm water creasing your legs with each gentle kick. Your bubbles seem softer, quieter. On the bottom you find a rock, sit down on it and turning off your light, notice the phosphorescence in the water as you move your hand. Looking up you notice you can see the moon and stars. Your bubbles float up as if they were on their way to these celestial bodies. You follow them. On the surface, alone, your eye follows the lights that dot the coastline of Maui. The dark outlines of Molokai and Lanai loom in the distance. For a moment time does not exist. But your dream is disrupted by the familiar sound of your dive buddies' regulators as they break the surface. Together everyone kicks for the beach.

This light from the sea may seem magical, yet many marine animals have the power to chemically generate light. This process is called bioluminescence. The disturbance caused by a wave of the hand excites the animals and causes them to emit light. Jellyfish, a variety of zooplankton, are particularly light-productive. Startled, small crustaceans will give off luminous clouds. Many squid and deep-sea shrimp emit a haze of luminous ink when threatened in order to confuse the enemy. The night sea, for those who are willing to venture and look, offers the experience of many lifetimes.

Night diving does require more skill than a daytime dive and training is a must and highly recommended. Once you're ready for that first open water ocean night dive, pick your spot carefully. Avoid all currents, rips, surf or other swift water condition. A calm full moon night is best. Find a beach

Photo courtesy of Cory Gray

your mind about the conditions or if the surf looks large, use common sense and abort the dive.

Night Diving

The full moon hanging over Lanai seems almost to turn night

alien underwater world presents itself to you. The concentration and diversity of sea life is inconceivable. Hidden by day, an eel now swims by seemingly unaware of your presence. Lobsters walk exposed on the ocean floor.

Instruction & Dive Data

with easy entry or dive from a well-anchored boat that is tended. Avoid deep dives, caves, wrecks and other underwater obstructions.

If you go from the shore you should leave a light burning at the point of departure. Two lights in-line will allow you to return to the exact spot with precision. Both lights should be amber, since many marine navigational aids are white, red or green.

When diving off a boat it's a good idea to have light on the boat and a light underwater on the anchor chain.

Use a chemical light attached to the snorkel or regulator valve so that you are visible when you're on the surface. These lights come in a twelve-hour variety. There is a high-intensity light which is 3-4 times brighter than general purpose, but lasts only for a short time.

As to the basic night diving equipment, it's the same as day plus a good diving light, a compass and a chemical light. It's a good idea to ensure your knife is with you, and you should carry a plastic whistle attached to your Buoyancy Compensator just in case you can't be seen from the boat. Pick your light carefully. Rechargeable lights are cheaper and brighter but tend not to burn as long as disposable dry cells. Make sure you use fresh batteries or that your rechargeable is fully charged. Back-up lights should be brought along as a precautionary measure.

Once you turn on to this new underwater experience you may want to improve the ability of a tender to see you by attaching a light reflective material - called SOLAS Grade Sheeting - to your wetsuit, hook, tank, snorkel or boat. This material has been coast guard tested and is said to be easily visible from a helicopter at 1500 feet, compared to 40 feet for an unmarked object.

As to the dangers at night, they really aren't too different from those during the day, although a close call can more readily create panic in the novice night diver. Don't let your body settle down on sea urchin spines. Shine your light into any holes you plan to stick your arm or body into. Eels may be swimming freely at night and should not bother you unless you box them into a crevice. Be careful of rays lying in depressions on the ocean bottom; swimming over them too closely may flush them out. Again, use your light to see what's in your path.

Lizard fish at Black Rock Point on Maui. Photo courtesy of Cory Gray

Instruction & Dive Data

Tips on Navigating at Night:

Use a compass.

- Watch depth: the farther out from shore, the deeper it is.
- Sand bottom ripples run parallel to shore.
- The moon is up, and so go your bubbles.
- The sound from the boat will be louder the closer you get.
- Use lights on shore and on boats.
- Best of all - know the area.

Remember:

1. Dive at night where you've been in the daytime. Know the area well. Plan your dive; dive your plan.

2. Know your light signals: Circle pattern, all OK. Rapid up and down pattern, help.

3. Don't shine your light in your buddy's face. Your eyes take a while to become accustomed to the dark. Turn off your light and you'll be amazed at how well you will still be able to make things out. You might try wearing dark or red sunglasses prior to a dive . . . just like pilots do.

4. It's good practice to follow the anchor chain to the bottom, stop and check all equipment, buddy up, then head out. Keep your compass bearing in mind and write on your slate.

5. As with any dive, avoid alcohol prior to the dive.

6. Avoid greasy or heavy foods.

7. Since it will still be dark and possibly cooler when you finish your dive, don't forget to bring along warm clothes.

8. If you get lost and separated from your buddy:

   a. Turn off your light; look for his chemical light.

   b. Surface and wait.

   c. Make sure your chemical light is visible.

   d. Scan the surface periodically with your main light - blow your whistle - don't panic.

Again, just imagine . . . a still, quiet, full moon night. You've seen more colors than ever, caressed sleeping fish, watched the characters of the deep out for a stroll and a bite to eat, each of them, just like humans, doing things at night they never do in the day!

Diamond Head. Photo by Warren Bolster, courtesy of Hawaii Visitors Bureau

PART VI
Diving Safety
&
Medicine

Photo courtesy of Cory Gray

DIVE SAFETY

If you are diving off the beach the entire burden of responsibility for safety will rely on you and your buddy. Hawaiian waters are riddled with hidden dangers: high surf, strong winds and currents. If you are going to dive a specific spot, get as much information as possible from a local dive shop as to when and where it is safe to dive. If you are unsure of yourself and want to dive with an instructor, ask about guided beach dives at the dive shop. If you are diving on your own off a private yacht you will want to take some extra safety precautions.

You may decide to dive off one of the many dive boats on the islands. These trips are highly supervised and the staff is very safety conscious. If you do decide to take the boat remember, even with a dive master present, the ultimate responsibility for your safety rests on your shoulders.

With all the responsibilities that a dive master carries, he or she has little time to be concerned about your personal diving profile. Usually the dive master plans the dives so that the first descent of the day is the deepest, followed by a shallow dive later, especially when the dives are separated by only an hour or two of surface interval.

Although planning the dives this way lessens potential problems, it is up to you to keep track of and record your own bottom time and maximum depth, and to calculate your repetitive dive status. These are important personal statistics that should be carefully noted in your log book. When it comes right down to the crunch, your personal safety is your responsibility.

Don't be afraid to question the dive master about the site or conditions if you are unsure, and know when you have reached the point where the diving conditions are beyond your abilities. It is better to miss a dive than end up in trouble under water. Most scuba enthusiasts packing for a diving holiday will think to include a basic maintenance and repair kit for their equipment. But often one piece of "gear" gets overlooked and that's you. Consider what preventive steps can be taken to ensure that you work properly while abroad.

Here are a few thoughts that may prove useful:

1. Try to rest for a day or two before your departure. Avoid overeating and excessive drinking during the flight. This helps minimize the effect of jet lag.

2. Allow your body to acclimatize before getting into non-stop diving, drinking, discos, etc. On the islands the humidity can be high with temperatures hanging at about 80 degrees day and night all year-round.

3. If you're diving on your own determine before you go where the nearest decompression chamber is located and what emergency procedures and transportation exist. Emergency air evaluation, chamber treatment and hospitalization can be extremely expensive so be sure your medical insurance is sufficient in both type and amount of coverage. Be sure to get all necessary receipts for medical treatment for proper claim documentation.

4. Be prepared to administer first aid. The objectives should be to sustain life, to prevent the condition from worsening and promote recovery. Attend a quality program in safety-oriented emergency first aid. It's invaluable knowledge to have all year-round. Be especially clear on procedures to follow in the event of any diving-related accident.

5. Always think preventive medicine. Flush out ears with clean, fresh water and dry them after every dive. Ear infections can start more easily in humid conditions. Treat all cuts and abrasions no matter how minor they might be. Don't let infections start.

6. Wear a "Medic Alert" bracelet or necklace if necessary. Traveling divers should also carry their own personal medical alert card at all times. Make it up on an index card and have it plasticized. Include name, address and telephone number of yourself, your next of kin and your doctor, medical/hospitalization insurance numbers and a brief medical history that includes allergies, diseases or conditions, prescription drugs used in past and present, special precautions to be taken in event of an emergency (i.e., check for contact lenses, avoid use of penicillin, etc.) and any other pertinent information.

HAND SIGNALS

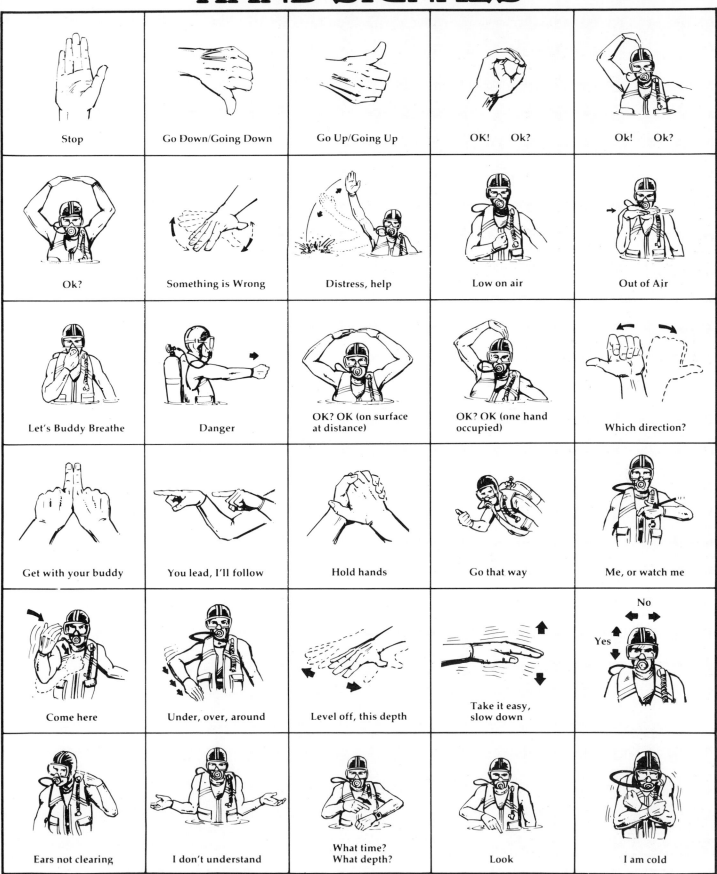

EQUIPMENT

EQUIPMENT MAINTENANCE
Pre-trip Checklist

MASKS: Check for cracks, or wear around buckle, and treat with preservative; buy a spare strap; check for any loose screws; pack and wrap carefully or keep in case to avoid scratching.

SNORKEL: Check for cracked or broken keeper; keep a spare keeper; attach mouthpiece firmly; look for cracks or tears; test easy movements of parts; check for air flow; mark tip with fluorescent or reflective tape.

FINS: Check for splitting or cracking of strap and fins; buy spare; treat with preservative.

BUOYANCY COMPENSATOR: Inflate and check for leaks in the bladder; check all valves for operation or sticking; lubricate all moving parts; lubricate inflator mechanism; check Velcro to ensure stitches are OK; check entire BC and straps for wear; ensure auto inflator mates properly and works. Make sure tank strap is working properly.

WETSUIT, SKIN SUIT, DIVE BAG ETC.: Check for wear, tears and split seams; check and lubricate all zippers especially on dive bag; check hood, boots, gloves.

REGULATOR: Check for corrosion or discoloration (if found, have checked by qualified professional); check for crack or wear, attach a full tank and test; check hose, hose fittings and second stage.

DIVE CONSOLE OR COMPUTER: Check for water leakage or corrosion (i.e. foggy lens); check pressure gauge against another; make sure needles are moving freely; check hose fittings.

DIVE KNIFE: Check for rust or corrosion; sharpen; lubricate with silicone grease; check ring and straps for cracking; buy extra ring and straps; treat with preservative.

DIVE LIGHT: Check for corrosion and good seals; replace batteries or charge; buy spare batteries and bulbs; check lanyard.

TANK: Check annually at shop for internal corrosion; check last hydrostatic date and do if needed; check valve for corrosion and smooth operation; turn off and submerge to check for leaks; check O-ring and get spares; remove boot and look for external corrosion; check tank pressure. (Tanks must be empty to be boarded on airplanes).

corrosion inside the regulator, or from the lubricant drying out, can cause tiny cracks, tears or splits, which eventually will break the seal completely.

How can you prevent these things from happening? No amount of washing or careful use can prevent your regulator from getting out of tune. Routine maintenance should be done every six months or once a year, depending on how often and where you dive. Generally, a good internal cleaning (ultrasonic or acid dip), by an experienced regulator repair technician, costs only about $35, and will take care of 90% of the performance problems.

Always, Always, Always...

- mark each piece of equipment.
- insure it under a household policy, having photographed it and recorded serial numbers, brand and identification marks, etc.

Never, Ever, Ever. . .

- use earplugs or goggles to dive under any circumstances. Earplugs make it impossible to equalize water pressure on both sides of the eardrum; the plugs could be forced into the outer ear canal, or an internal squeeze could result. There is no way of equalizing pressure inside goggles; at increasing depths, the goggles squeeze into the flesh, forcing out the eyes . . . .

And, we're talking pain.

Regular Maintenance Diagnosis Tips

"What if...?

. . . You experience hard breathing with your regulator! Most likely saltwater has corroded it, and the internal moving parts, which have become encrusted and scaled, now stick or operate sluggishly. Rust clogging of the first stage's sintered filter, or

carbon dust clogging also create resistance to smooth airflow.

. . . Your regulator mouthpiece leaks water! No doubt the second stage exhalation valve has deteriorated, from chlorinated water, ozone or normal aging. If it slows, dirt, sand or dust particles may have irreversibly marred or dented the high pressure valve seat in the first stage.

. . . Your O-rings leak! Build up of salt

Flags

North Americans have learned to respond to a red square, divided diagonally by a white bar, to mean "diver down," and legislative efforts to convert them to recognizing the international blue and white symbol have been disbanded recently. Either flag should be displayed, stiffened on a float, and boaters should respond by keeping clear by at least 100 feet, and by slowing down. Divers should always surface within 50 feet of their flags.

Diving Safety & Medicine

How to Pack Gear For Travel

There are a lot of different gear-packing strategies adopted over the years by traveling divers. Some suggest using a "whale-sized" dive bag. The idea here is if you are packing for two, this can be a good idea, as a seventy-pound bag is less likely to appeal to thieves than two more easily lifted bags. Small locks on the zippers of the dive bags can also provide at least some small resistance to someone who maybe isn't totally committed to stealing your dive gear. Some divers place their gear in a large suitcase concealing the dive gear now disguised as normal luggage. The only problem here is that when you go diving you won't have a dive bag to haul your gear around in.

Packing the gear efficiently can also prove a challenge. If you don't have separate pockets for your fins place them in the bag first, to help protect the rest of the gear from beneath, then put the suits in.

Take your own BC and regulator. Using your own equipment on a trip means that you are better able to concentrate on getting good pictures instead of fiddling around with unfamiliar dive gear. Bring a weight belt but leave the weights at home. Be sure to note how much weight is on your belt as you remove the lead. Protect your console gauges by putting them into booties and packing them in the center of the bag. The same goes for the regulators. If you have a large dive bag, use a couple of good straps around the bag. If the zipper goes, the contents will stay in place. Always carry your prescription masks with you.

Basic Maintenance

1. Rinse equipment in warm, rather than cold, water to help dissolve accumulated salt. Rinse the regulator's second stage under a stream of fresh water, allowing it to run freely through any open ports, but do not purge the button.

2. Minimize exposure to the sun of neoprene rubber items, such as masks, snorkels and fins; also chlorine and ozone. Keep them away from paint, gas fumes and suntan lotions.

3. Use silicone spray sparingly, and never on regulators.

4. Store equipment at a constant temperature, away from smog and electric motors. For extended periods dry thoroughly and seal in plastic bags.

5. Care for rips, fraying, sticking valves, rust, etc. as they appear.

6. Regularly have gear professionally checked. Never disassemble a regulator yourself.

Equipment Check List

General Equipment
- Regulator with pressure
  gauge and extra second stage
- Console or computer
- Compass
- Knife
- Light
- Dive tables
- Slate with pencil
- Lights (chemical)PML

Suit Up
- Mask and snorkel
- Fins
- Gloves
- Boots
- Wetsuit or skinsuit
- B.C.
- Dive flag and float
- Gear line
- First aid kit

Carry-on Equipment
- Weight belt & weights
- Tank

Spare
- Mask straps
- Fin straps
- O-rings and batteries
- Bulbs
- Silicone spray
- Knife strap

Personal
- Watch
- Swimsuit
- Towel
- Hat
- Jacket
- Sunglasses
- C-card
- Money and fishing license
- Log book
- Sunscreen
- Skin lotions
- Motion sickness medication
- Insect repellant
- Change of clothes

Diving Safety & Medicine

A number of dive boats operate out of Lahaina on Maui giving divers access to islands like Lanai and Molokini Crater. Photo courtesy of Rick Baker

ADAPTING
TO THE MARINE ENVIRONMENT

The scope of changes you undergo while diving is far more extensive than most people realize. Environmental changes in visibility, temperature, pressure, water movement and bottom conditions are obvious. But physiological changes in heart rate, blood pressure, respiration, temperature, stress fatigue and body weight are taking place, and all senses are significantly altered. So how do people not only survive, but accomplish so much underwater?

Be Cool, Stay Warm

Underwater adaptation usually comes first with special equipment and skills, then with training and experience. The skills are essentially the same.

Capable divers:

- move in a slow and relaxed manner
- move through the water in a horizontal attitude
- only move arms and legs when necessary
- often crawl along the bottom, gently using fingers and fin tips rather than swimming
- avoid surface swimming as much as possible
- breathe in a slow, deep, relaxed manner and often pause during the dive
- control buoyancy to be neutral or just slightly negative when moving horizontally in midwater
- slightly negative when on the bottom or descending,
- and positive when ascending or on the surface
- use natural aids to underwater orientation and navigation
- stop, breathe easily, think and get control before taking action during difficulty
- solve problems on the bottom if possible, or on the surface using positive buoyancy
- end or modify dives when they are cold, tired, low on air, not feeling well, having a difficulty, injured, uncomfortable, under stress, or not having a good time
- always surface slowly and never rush to exit point
- make equipment and water movement work for them
- are aware of themselves, the equipment and their surroundings
- recognize and deal with stress; are able to coordinate several skills at once: such as equalizing pressure, controlling buoyancy and swimming

Don't Be A Drag

Moving efficiently through the water is a very important aspect of adaptation. In order to dive, however, you must be equipped with the appropriate gear, which creates a lot of water resistance.

Some equipment-related causes of drag are:

- large, bulky gear
- dangling or protruding accessories
- drysuits, especially when inflated
- irregular or flat surfaces
- extra equipment such as camera

Some procedures that increase drag are:

- swimming out of trim
- excessively inflating a buoyancy compensator
- kicking with excessively bent legs, using hands to maneuver
- swimming fast
- swimming on the surface

What to do instead?

- use simplest equipment available for type of diving you do
- streamline equipment
- carry as little as possible
- secure everything
- wear as complete and smooth an exposure suit as possible
- maintain neutral buoyancy and horizontal trim
- use an efficient kick
- swim at a slow, steady pace
- swim on the surface as little as possible
- use water currents or surge to propel yourself
- crawl along bottom
- use buoyancy control for ascents and descents

Finally what does all this achieve for the diver? It improves safety and enjoyment of the sport. It is clear that you use less air and become less fatigued moving efficiently through the water, and you will see more, be less cold, be under less stress, not have as many difficulties and will be better able to keep a sense of orientation.

Lion fish at Black Rock Point on Maui. Photo courtesy of Cory Gray

DIVING ACCIDENTS

Some Causes

A familiar chain of events often appears: the diver is cold and tired. Stress levels increase, and the diver makes a mistake. He panics and dies. The key link in this chain is the mistake or human error that may have been anything from entering heavy surf to not properly maintaining a regulator.

Human Error

This stands out as the primary cause of the vast majority of diving accidents. The largest single category of causes, however, is that of medical and psychological factors. These include problems of stress and panic, cold and fatigue, cramps, drug abuse (including alcohol), decompression sickness, contaminated air, heart conditions and other medical problems, along with poor physical and psychological fitness.

Either by their behavior or by allowing things to happen to them, people cause the problems that lead to diving accidents.

Environmental Conditions

Another large group of causative factors include environmental conditions such as deep water, waves, currents, cold water, poor visibility, entanglements, and so on. Some divers attempt to blame accidents that involve environmental conditions on "acts of God," or claim that conditions are beyond their control. Yet the divers chose to dive in these conditions, or the conditions changed and the divers chose not to deal effectively with them. In any case, it generally leads back to human error.

Equipment Failure

Ascent difficulties occurring after "out of air" and "low on air" situations are a type of accident unique to sport diving. Actually, the error is one of equipment misuse or improper breathing procedures — both human errors. Equipment failure is insignificant as a primal cause of fatal scuba diving accidents. Equipment can cause problems, but is more likely to inconvenience the diver than threaten his life. The accident also may be caused by the diver's misuse of the equipment. Other major problem areas are the failure of the buddy system, lack of buoyancy control and lack of training – again, all human errors.

Key Trends

Other trends in scuba diving accidents show that on a dive-for-dive basis the earliest dives (first dozen) in a person's diving career are most likely to lead to difficulties. Also, nearly all fatal accidents occur while using scuba in open water. But an accident is most likely to be a near miss if qualified people such as instructors, guides, dive masters or boat crews are readily available.

Putting these trends together indicates that sport divers should dive with professionally qualified people or in supervised activities while gaining their early experience. This would also be a wise recommendation for anyone who has been away from diving for several months.

Learning Control

Develop the ability to make the no-dive decision based on changing medical, physical, psychological or environmental conditions. Along with this goes the right for either diver at any time to abort the dive without embarrassment. Divers should get out of the water when they are cold, tired, low on air, under undue stress, injured, uncomfortable or having difficulty. Diving is not enjoyable or safe under these conditions.

If you are having difficulties during a dive, it is best to stop, think and get control. Then take corrective action. Use your equipment to help control buoyancy and maintain orientation. Diving is a demanding activity, but an extremely rewarding one. The key to enjoyment is control. Maintain control of yourself, your equipment, and the situation so you and your buddy can function within the existing conditions, whatever they may be.

Diving Safety & Medicine

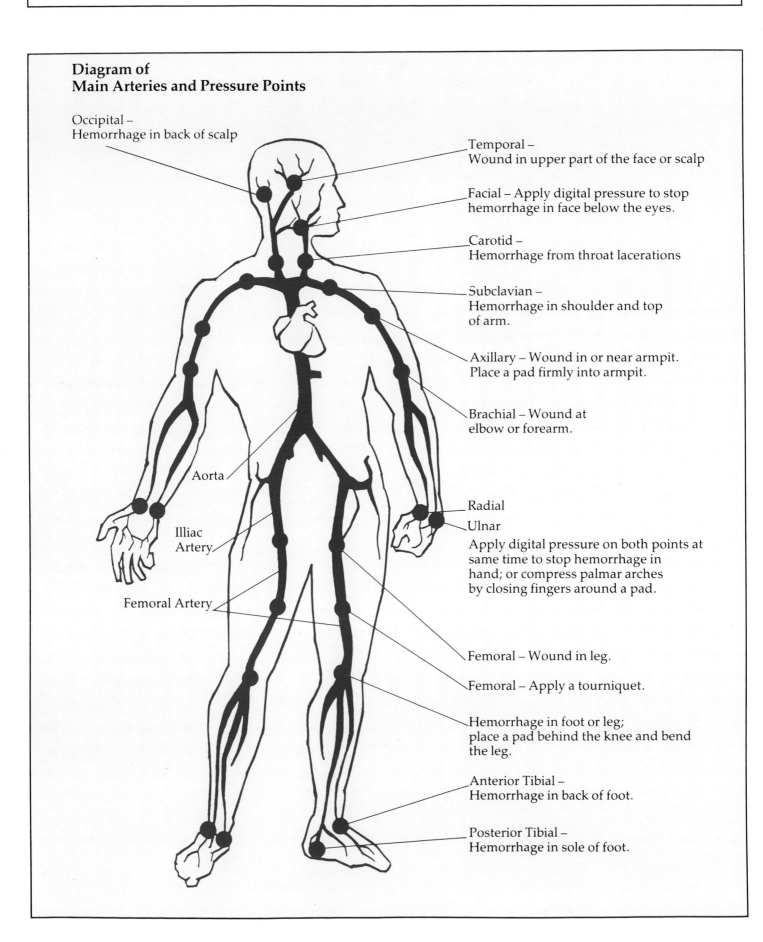

**Diagram of
Main Arteries and Pressure Points**

Occipital –
Hemorrhage in back of scalp

Temporal –
Wound in upper part of the face or scalp

Facial – Apply digital pressure to stop
hemorrhage in face below the eyes.

Carotid –
Hemorrhage from throat lacerations

Subclavian –
Hemorrhage in shoulder and top
of arm.

Axillary – Wound in or near armpit.
Place a pad firmly into armpit.

Brachial – Wound at
elbow or forearm.

Aorta

Radial

Ulnar

Illiac
Artery

Apply digital pressure on both points at
same time to stop hemorrhage in
hand; or compress palmar arches
by closing fingers around a pad.

Femoral Artery

Femoral – Wound in leg.

Femoral – Apply a tourniquet.

Hemorrhage in foot or leg;
place a pad behind the knee and bend
the leg.

Anterior Tibial –
Hemorrhage in back of foot.

Posterior Tibial –
Hemorrhage in sole of foot.

Tips for Treatment of Injuries

There are numerous good first aid manuals available which are quite adequate for treatment of common injuries. This section will attempt to outline the first aid for minor injuries specific to diving or snorkeling.

EXTERNAL EAR CANAL INFECTION (Swimmer's ear)

Signs/Symptoms: Pain, redness, tenderness of outer ear, discharge from ear canal.

Treatment: Prevent - Avoid trauma (Q-tips, etc.) Vinegar/alcohol drops after diving/swimming, or boric acid 3% plus 70% isopropyl alcohol - 50/50 mix.

Clear ear canal (ENT specialist): Cortisporin drops.
See First Aid Kit.

SINUS SQUEEZE

S and SX: Pain in sinuses, nosebleed.

Treatment: Prevent - Don't dive with a cold, clear sinuses, topical and oral decongestants 30 minutes before dive.

Treatment - Don't dive until Sx clear, decongestants (Afrin spray), Sudafed (120 mg SA capsule twice daily) steroids.

EAR SQUEEZE

S and SX: Pain in ear, headache, dizziness, vomiting, hearing loss if rupture of ear drum. The most common cause of diving accidents.

Treatment: Prevention - Same as sinus squeeze.
Treatment - Same as sinus squeeze. If rupture of eardrum or severe symptoms see ENT specialist.

STINGS (Jellyfish, Fire Coral, sea anemones, bristle worms, starfish). Sea cucumbers can ingest toxic hydroids and may cause stings, with possible blindness resulting.

Signs and Symptoms: Wide range: welts, swelling, redness, numbness of skin, pain (mild – severe), cramps, nausea/vomiting, respiratory difficulty, paralysis, convulsions and shock.

Prevention: Avoid touching animals, including dead jellyfish on beach.

Treatment:

1. Remove victim from water.
2. Treat for shock and respiratory collapse.
3. Rinse with sea water (not fresh water), then with 70% alcohol or ammonia solution (vodka or shaving lotion in a pinch).
4. Apply paste of Adolf's meat tenderizer or bicarbonate/alcohol or bicarb/ammonia (or shaving lotion in a pinch).
5. Cortisone cream (0.5% available without prescription).
6. Seek medical help for severe cases.

7. Remove bristle worm bristles with adhesive tape.
8. Ice packs to reduce swelling and pain.

NOTE: Man-O-War stings require immediate treatment.

SEA URCHIN/VENOMOUS SPINES

Symptoms: Pain, swelling, blanching or redness (infection) or granules (late).

Prevention: Avoid, wear protection.

Treatment: Remove spines with sterile needle/forceps, wash with antiseptic, apply ammonia solution.

VENOMOUS FISH (Scorpionfish, turkeyfish, lionfish, etc.)

Symptoms: Pain at puncture site, blanching, swelling, redness, dizziness, nausea, respiratory problems, pulse alterations, shock, coma, death.

Prevention: Avoid, wear protection.

Treatment: Remove from water. Remove spines, foreign material. KEY: Soak injured area in HOT water (110-115 deg F or 43-46 deg C) for 45 to 90 minutes. Relieve pain (narcotics are usually necessary). Cleanse wound. Seek medical attention.

DANGEROUS FISH BITES (sharks, barracuda, moray eel)

Symptoms: Laceration, may be severe; victim usually dies from blood loss and shock.

Prevention: Avoid; sharks are ubiquitous and unpredictable, greatest danger to surface swimmers. Slowly leave water if dangerous shark sighted.

Treatment:

1. Control bleeding (direct pressure; tourniquet only if absolutely necessary; loosen every 20 minutes).
2. CPR if necessary.
3. Remove from water.
4. Treat shock (head down; warm; IV fluids, if available).
5. Seek immediate medical attention.

BARNACLE OR CORAL CUTS/ABRASION

Treatment: Cleanse thoroughly with betadine/H2O2. Apply Betadine or Neosporin ointment. See physician for signs of infection.

SUNBURN

Symptoms: Redness, pain, swelling, blister formation of skin.

KEY-Prevention: Protective clothing, increase time in sun gradually; use sunscreen with SPF 8-15 containing PABA 5% in alcohol or water-resistant base.

Treatment: Avoid further exposure, cool compresses, aspirin, cortisone creams if severe.

Diver's First Aid Kit

Several pre-packaged first aid kits are available commercially today. These vary from poor to excellent when utilized for diving-related accidents. The following list has been compiled for those who wish to either save a few dollars or customize a kit, and start with the basic necessities. As new products become available, the kit should be updated. Don't forget to restock used items. Most items are available from your local drug store. Prescription drugs are marked with an (*) and should be obtained through your personal physician.

1. One-Tackle/Tool Box as a container. Plastic or metal. The Pelican Camera Box is ideal although quite expensive.
2. Adhesive Tape/Assorted Bandages. Cloth or silk tape is best.
3. Alcohol Solution. 70% to 95% isopropyl.
4. Ammonia Solution. Useful for treating stings.
5. Antibiotic Ointment. Betadine, Neosporin.
6. Antibiotic Powder. Neosporin.
7. Antihistamines. (Benadryl*) Oral, (injectable)
8. Aspirin. Useful for sinus squeeze headaches, fevers as well as decompression sickness.
9. Assorted Dressings. 4 x 4 sterile gauzes, roll gauze 4" x 5 yd., Non-adherent (Telfa, Adaptic).
10. Baking Soda.
11. Decongestant. Oral (Sudafed +), + 120mg SA Recomm Topical (Afrin nasal spray).
12. Diarrhea Medications. (Lomotil*, Pepto Bismol (Septra*).
13. Dive Tables. An extra copy of the tables should be included as a backup and can be used in the event of an emergency.
14. Ear Drops. Vinegar 1 tbsp. in 4 oz. 70% alcohol or 3% boric acid in 70% alcohol 50:50; Cortisporin*.
15. Emergency Numbers. Make up a self-adhering sticker with emergency numbers for your area on it. Include the National Diving Accident Network (DAN) Phone number (919) 684-8111. U.S. Coast Guard (at sea VHF 16), local rescue number and the number of the nearest decompression chamber. Also tape dimes (2) and quarters (2) to lid for phone calls.
16. Eye Drops. 10% Sulfacetamide*, Neosporin.
17. Flashlight. Include extra batteries and bulbs. Disposable penlights work well, are compact and inexpensive.
18. Hydrogen Peroxide. (H202) for wound cleansing.
19. Ice Packs. To reduce swelling/pain. Instant wet/dry mixture which are activated by squeezing are best.
20. Insect Repellant. (Cutters, Off).
21. Meat Tenderizer. (Containing Papain) Adolf's Unseasoned. Use for jelly fish and coral stings.
22. Oxygen. With appropriate device for administration. Should be available for treatment of DCS or gas embolism.
23. Pain Medication. (Aspirin, Tylenol, Narcotics*).
24. Pencil, Pen and Paper. Include a standard and a grease pencil for documentation of changes in a diver's condition, times, instructions from rescue/medical personnel, etc.
25. Saline Solution. 0.9 saline (Na Cl) is the normal physiologic concentration. Can be used for anything from burns to ear/eye flushes. If not available contact lens solution may be used; assure that it does not contain irritants.
26. Scissors and forceps (tweezers). A good quality stainless steel set is well worth the money. They will stay sharp and won't rust. Forceps are useful for sea urchin spine removal.
27. Scrub Brush.
28. Soap Antiseptic Scrub. Betadine, Hibiclens for cleaning wounds.
29. Sun Screen. Should contain PABA in alcohol base.
30. Sea Sickness Medication. Transderm Scop*, Dramamine, Bonine, Marazine.
31. Space Blanket. Packaged foil blankets work well and take up little space. Available at sporting goods or drug store.
32. Thermometer. A must. Preferable is one that will read in hypothermic range.
33. Triangular Bandage. Use for a sling or to control bleeding.
34. Tourniquet. Know how to use and indications!
35. The kit should also contain important prescription medications by the diver on an individual basis.
++ Drugs such as injectable cortisone or adrenalin may also be included but generally should be administered under the auspices of a physician.

Thermal Conductivity Is 24 Times Greater In Water Than In Air

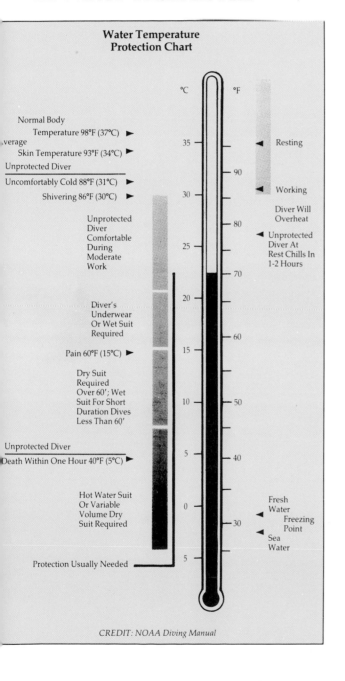

Water Temperature Protection Chart

°C °F

Normal Body Temperature 98°F (37°C) ▶
Average
Skin Temperature 93°F (34°C) ▶
Unprotected Diver

Uncomfortably Cold 88°F (31°C) ▶
Shivering 86°F (30°C) ▶

35 — ◀ Resting

90 —

30 — ◀ Working

Diver Will Overheat

Unprotected Diver Comfortable During Moderate Work

80 —
25 —
◀ Unprotected Diver At Rest Chills In 1-2 Hours

70 —

Diver's Underwear Or Wet Suit Required

20 —

Pain 60°F (15°C) ▶

15 — 60 —

Dry Suit Required Over 60'; Wet Suit For Short Duration Dives Less Than 60'

10 — 50 —

Unprotected Diver
Death Within One Hour 40°F (5°C) ▶

5 — 40 —

Hot Water Suit Or Variable Volume Dry Suit Required

0 —
Fresh Water ◀ Freezing Point
30 — ◀ Sea Water

Protection Usually Needed

5 —

CREDIT: NOAA Diving Manual

Seasickness

This poorly understood malady has not only ruined many a dive or fishing trip, it has probably changed the course of history. Most assuredly, some of the greatest sea captains and admirals have been seriously afflicted. Almost everyone, at some time or another, is susceptible, especially if unaccustomed to the erratic rocking motions of a boat in open water. Motion sickness is caused by discordant stimuli to the part of the inner ear which controls balance. Factors contributing to motion sickness are genetic susceptibility, age, sex, prior evening's activities, previous meals, noxious stimuli (engine exhaust) and emotional factors. There is some adaptation in most people: that is, symptoms may decrease with repeated stimulation - a positive note! There are as many ways to prevent seasickness as there are cures, and none are completely successful. Depending on your background, you may have tried various herbs, including garlic and ginger, vitamins (B6 was recently touted by the Russians), wearing of various charms, eating, not eating, and numerous drugs. If one is faced with impending symptoms, he should move to the boat's centerline, amidship, as close to the waterline as possible to minimize motion stimulus. Look at the horizon or shut your eyes and sleep, if possible. Avoid engine exhaust and other adverse sensory input. Don't repeatedly console or chide others who are afflicted; this only makes things worse! Frequently, getting in the water as soon as possible helps.

For those highly susceptible to motion sickness, attention should be given to three things: prior night's activities, diet, and medications which block or prevent symptoms. A good night's rest, and absence of a hangover, will help greatly to minimize chances for motion sickness. Your diet should be light, low in fat and acid or gas producing foods. Eat three or four hours before the dive. Of the numerous medications used, Scopolamine is probably the most effective. Available in a skin patch (Trans-derm Scop), it is available by prescription only and should be tried prior to diving to assess severity of side effects, which may include dry mouth, drowsiness, blurred vision and hallucinations. Over the counter drugs include Dramamine, Marezine, and Bonine - all antihistamine derivatives which vary in results, duration and side effects. Other prescription medications such as Phenergan, alone or in combination, should probably be avoided when diving because of possible side effects. Although getting into the water quickly may abort an attack, one should not scuba dive if severely seasick. The cause of motion sickness is still somewhat of a mystery. If the above measures are ineffective, the best advice is to avoid rough weather in a boat and to keep tabs on the latest medical advances either through publications or one's physician.

Drugs and Diving

Drugs and scuba diving don't mix. In a culture which is drug-oriented, chemicals are used for prevention and cure of every malady, from the common cold to cancer. For the scuba diver, many drugs are effective and safe on the surface, but at depth, side effects may be serious and even dangerous. Several categories should be mentioned. They are summarized in Table A. These are: analgesics, antihistamines and decongestants, anti-nausea drugs, cardiovascular drugs, anticonvulsants, sedatives, stimulants and abused or street drugs.

It is generally accepted that persons with seizures, asthma, diabetes, serious cardiovascular or psychological disorders requiring medication should not dive. On the other hand, commonly used drugs such as caffeine, aspirin and Tylenol ordinarily do not jeopardize divers. Without question, abused, mind-altering substances such as cocaine, marijuana, alcohol, amphetamines, narcotics, downers, minor tranquilizers, (Valium, etc.) and sedatives like Quaaludes, do not mix with diving and are dangerous, even on the surface.

Decongestants are probably the most commonly used medications for the diver. Although they are stimulants, and can cause disturbances in heart rhythms, medications such as Sudafed are considered safe in the healthy diver. The 60 mg tablet should be taken about 30 minutes before diving; Sudafed-SA capsules are recommended if delays or repetitive dives are contemplated as they may prevent reverse squeezes.

Antihistamines cause sedation, and should be used with caution. Topical decongestants, such as Afrin nasal spray, are safe but can cause a type of dependence if overused.

Anti-nauseants all cause sedation to some extent, as well as other side-effects, which may cause nitrogen narcosis. Always test topside and use with caution. Shallow dives of less than 60 feet are recommended. Cardiovascular drugs include beta-blockers, such as Inderal, which decrease one's ability to handle stress. Antihypertensives, which lower blood pressure, have numerous serious side-effects. It is prudent to say that patients requiring these medications should not be diving at depth, both because of the underlying disease process and the medication involved. However, each case can be individualized. A physician knowledgeable in the effects of pressure should be consulted in these patients. Diuretics (water pills) are usually okay. Of the abused drugs, alcohol is the most common. It is a depressant and involved in about one-half of adult drownings. In addition, the dehydration effect can make decompression sickness worse, and heat loss is increased, adding to hypothermia. Marijuana is an extremely dangerous drug at depth, causing many "bad trips" through paradoxical effects and severe cold intolerance. Other mind-altering substances cause greatly impaired performance and altered perceptions, all of which are increased at pressure. Diving creates enough of a "high" itself. Use of these substances is only to be condemned.

Coral formation at Honolua Bay on Maui. Photo courtesy of Cory Gray

---

TABLE A
Drugs & Diving

SAFE DRUGS (OK to Dive)	NO DIVING	RESTRICTED DIVING (With Caution)
	Anti-convulsants	
Aspirin	Asthma medications	Antihistamines
Acetaminophen	Antihypertensives	Decongestants
(Tylenol, others)	Alcohol	Anti-motion sickness
Caffeine	Depressants	medications
Topical decongestants	(Barbituates, etc.)	Steroids
	Stimulants	
	(amphetamines, Cocaine)	
	Hallucinogens	
	(Marijuana, LSD, PCP, Mescaline, etc.)	
	Tranquilizers	
	Antipyschotic medications	
	Narcotics	

NOTE: When taking any drug and diving, REMEMBER to consider whether the condition itself is hazardous when diving.

Diving Safety & Medicine

Ropes & Knots

A variety of natural and synthetic fibers are used to make rope. All rope materials have characteristics which can be either an advantage or disadvantage, depending upon how the rope is used. Nylon, for example, is very elastic; it is great for towing boats. Because of its elasticity, though, it can snap with tremendous force when its breaking strength is exceeded.

The knot you use for a job is partly determined by the type of rope you have. A knot that holds fast in manilla rope may untie in nylon. Ropes are tools. They will serve you well if you know how to use and treat them. Knowing when and how to tie the knots described here should help you be an asset to any dive team.

KNOT TYING TERMS
End – loose or working part of a rope.
Bight – a curve in a rope or line; usually where the knot is tied.
Standing Part – unused section of rope in knot tying.
Loop – a closed curve in a rope or line.

1. The figure eight knot is most often used as a stopper knot. It is used more than the overhand knot because the figure eight does not tighten as much under pressure.

2. Square knot. This knot is used to tie rope ends of the same size together. It is a quick way to join rope, but since it reduces rope strength by almost 50%, it should not be used under great tension.

3. Two-half hitches. Easy to tie and effective, two-half hitches are used to secure line to a stationary point or grommets.

4. Rolling hitch. When you cannot afford to have a rope slip sideways on a rail or rope, use a rolling hitch. The rolling hitch is also good for tying a line to a rope secured (attached) at both ends.

5. Bowline. Every diver needs this knot. It is easy to tie with a little practice. Use it any time a loop is needed at the end of a line.

Ropes & Knots

6. Ring knot. The ring knot can be tied when you have to join two ropes in a hurry. Keep in mind it can jam under a moderate strain.

7. Sheetbend. This knot is recommended for tying the ends of two ropes together to make a longer rope.

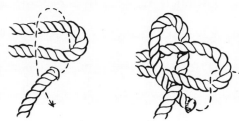 

8. Double Sheetbend. This one can take more strain than the sheetbend without jamming. It is highly recommended for tying ropes of different diameters together.

9. Bowline Bend. This knot is two bowlines which interlock. It can also be used to tie ropes of different diameters together. It is the preferred knot when a boat or vehicle has to be towed.

10. Sheepshank. When a shorter rope is needed, or a weak spot in the line has to be strengthened, tie a sheepshank.

11. Slipped overhand knot. This knot is ideal for a temporary stopper knot. To untie it, simply pull at the end.

The Effects of Pressure

These are the most interesting and significant external phenomenon that affect the physiology of the scuba diver. The tissues of the body as well as the surrounding liquid of the oceans follow the gas laws of physics and account for many of the medical problems encountered by those venturing into the deep. Basically, these (collectively known as "bubble trouble") fall into two categories: those due to direct effects of pressure and those secondary effects. They are the most common diving malady encountered and have a wide range of severity. Direct effects of ambient pressure are mechanical in nature and, in accordance with Boyle's law (volume at depth is inversely proportional to pressure), may cause difficulty during descent (ear, sinus or lung squeeze) or during ascent (pulmonary overpressure accidents such as the middle ear or sinus) when surrounding pressure exceeds that of the space through failure of equalization. This causes swelling, engorgement and eventual rupture of blood vessels and can result in severe pain and other symptoms. Reverse squeeze is usually the result of poor timing of a dose of decongestant. The diver clears easily during descent but, because the medication taken too early wears off at depth, clearing is impossible during ascent. This can result in incredible pain, eardrum rupture, etc. If decongestants must be taken, use the long acting type and never dive with a cold. Lung squeeze is a problem only in very deep breath-hold diving and is rarely encountered in the sport scuba diver.

Pulmonary overpressure accidents (POA), also termed air or gas emboli, are a second, and potentially more serious class of diving accidents, caused by the mechanical effects of pressure. They can occur only if a breath is taken beneath the surface (compressed air tank, air pocket of wreck, etc.) and the expanding air cannot be normally vented during ascent to the surface. This blockage is usually the result of breath holding but may be caused by local air trapping in a defective lung. Asthmatics, smokers and those with congenital lung blebs are at an increased risk. The increasing pressure causes rupture of the delicate air sacs (alveoli), or pleural lining, and gas bubbles are forced into the circulation. The disastrous symptoms outlined in Table A are usually very serious,

causing more deaths in a compressed air diver than any other pressure phenomenon. POA can usually be prevented by normal breathing (not forced exhalation) during ascent. It is important to remember that emboli can occur at depths of less than four feet of seawater. Most POA's are potentially serious and require decompression in a suitable hyperbaric chamber. Indirect effects of pressure follow the laws of Dalton (total pressure exerted in a gas is equal to the sum of the partial pressures of each individual gas) and Henry (the amount of gas dissolved in a liquid is proportional to the partial pressure of that gas) and explain disorders such as decompression sickness (DCS, "bends") and nitrogen narcosis. At depth tissues may become saturated with

Photo courtesy of Cory Gray

dissolved inert gases (e.g. nitrogen). If barometric pressure is lowered too rapidly, the gas separates from the liquid medium and forms bubbles in blood or other tissues. This evokes a complex series of chemical changes which result in the various DCS syndromes.

Treatment of DCS are outlined in Table B and Fig. 1. REMEMBER: Any symptom, including that of joint pain or extreme fatigue, following compressed air diving is considered serious and should be treated aggressively. Mild symptoms often progress to more serious ones.

A second effect of indirect pressure is that of nitrogen narcosis, or, as Cousteau termed, "rapture of the deep." This may occur at depths of much less than 100 feet, and is greatly potentiated by various drugs as well as individual and day-to-day variation among divers.

REMEMBER: the Martini Rule: Each 50 feet depth = one Martini. Contamination of breathing air with carbon monoxide, etc., may be influenced by pressure changes only.

Flying After Diving

If you fly too soon after diving, you could be in for a painful, if not dangerous, experience. Excess nitrogen remaining in your system can cause decompression sickness (bends) that would not occur at sea level. Reduced pressure does exist in modern jets flying at high altitude. That's why our ears pop. Commercial aircraft are only pressurized to a maximum of 8,000 feet above sea level. Problems with flying after diving, at such reduced pressures, are obvious. A similar condition to diving at altitude would exist, and similar precautions should be made. Remember, bends have occurred merely by driving over mountains after diving. Recommendations by the Undersea Medical Society include: (1) For no-decompression dives, when total bottom time for all dives in the preceding 12 hours is less than one hour ("D diver"), wait at least four hours before flying in a commercial jet. (2) If bottom time is four hours or less, wait at least 12 hours. (3) If more than four hours have been spent in the water in the previous 12, you should wait at least 24 hours before flying.

If symptoms do develop during your flight home, notify the flight crew immediately. One hundred percent oxygen should be given and cabin pressure increased, if possible. Emergency landing may be necessary if symptoms persist. Here again, prevention is the best cure. Planning a day of topside activities the last day of your diving vacation is the recommended way to prevent "bubble trouble" on your flight home.

Cramps

Divers, like runners and other athletes who use their legs a lot, are subject to cramps, usually from one of three causes. Your body could be lacking some nutrient, usually potassium. Eating bananas can increase your potassium intake. More than likely, though, you're out of condition. A good exercise program, begun several weeks before your expected dive, can help. You should check out several routines used by runners, whereby you stretch your leg muscles prior to diving. The last major cause is improper kicking. Have a buddy check your kick. If you're bending your knees in a "bicycle type" kick, you're putting undue stress on muscles. A good kick should be slow and long-sweeping, moving from the hips. Once you're kicking correctly, begin a regular routine of practice. If problems persist, have a doctor check you over, just to be on the safe side.

Pregnancy and Diving

In 1980 a workshop was held by the Undersea Medical Society (UMS). The findings suggest that even though the expectant mother doesn't experience any decompression problems, the fetus might. Also, if the expectant mother does need decompression, the common practice of treatment with 100% oxygen can harm the fetus. The UMS recommendation is that pregnant women refrain from diving. Perhaps while in care of this new life, an expectant mother should practice her surface snorkeling skills only and wait until after the birth to introduce her young to the joys of scuba. Japanese female pearl divers have almost three times the rate of premature births as compared to non-diving women. On the other hand, there have been anecdotal reports of healthy infants born to mothers who have dived extensively during pregnancy. Species differences and experimental technique differences account for some of the conflicting research results. There are ongoing studies which will hopefully elucidate this important problem; however, until accurate information is available, the recommendations of the Undersea Medical Society should be followed. That is, prospective moms in charge of a new life practice their snorkeling skills, soak up the sun and wait until after the birth to enjoy the pleasures of scuba.

Divers Alert Network
Making Diving Safer for You

The Divers Alert Network (DAN) is a non-profit member-supported diving safety organization based at Duke University Medical Center.

Since 1980, DAN has made diving safer by arranging medical consultation for injured divers, collecting and analyzing diving accidents and fatalities, providing diving safety programs, and offering diving accident insurance and air evacuations.

DAN offers the following services:

Telephone Hotlines

DAN maintains a 24-hour emergency hotline and medical information line. Divers anywhere can call and receive the latest information about diving safety or can arrange for transportation and treatment to a diving physician or medical facility.

Emergency Hotline — (919) 684-8111
This hotline provides a central location for diving emergency coordination. It unites diving physicians and hyperbaric chamber facilities into a nationwide communications network, 24 hours a day. DAN handles about 1,500 emergency calls a year.

Medical Information — (919) 684-2948
This information line is operated from 9 a.m. to 5 p.m. ET, Monday through Friday, by medical personnel specially trained in diving medicine. DAN handles an increasing number of information calls per year. In 1991 DAN answered over 12,000 calls.

Dive Accident Insurance

DAN Prepared Members receive worldwide diving accident insurance for any in-water injury. This secondary insurance covers up to $15,000 (or $30,000 coverage for only $5 more) for treatment of diving-related injuries.

Assist America

DAN provides free global emergency evacuation assistance for all DAN members and their families through Assist America.

Any DAN member, whether insured or not, can be evacuated from anywhere in the world to an appropriate medical facility in the event of an accident or illness at no cost! The accident does not have to be dive related.

Alert Diver

Alert Diver is the official bimonthly magazine of DAN. Alert Diver has the latest information about diving and medicine. It also features regular columns about medications, seminars, and case histories.

Accident & Fatality Report

DAN publishes a comprehensive annual Report on Diving Accidents and Fatalities. It is available for $15.

Diving Safety Courses

Hundreds of divers have benefited from DAN's One Day Diving Safety Seminar. Diverse groups from dive clubs to rescue teams have sponsored this informative seminar. These courses are accredited and offer continuing medical education hours for medical professionals.

DAN also offers many instructional books, videos, and tapes for individuals and clubs.

Oxygen First Aid in Dive Accidents

The use of oxygen to treat injured divers has long been recognized as one of the best measures for a successful recovery. DAN offers basic provider and oxygen instructor courses. These courses are recommended by all the major training organizations.

Joining DAN

When an individual joins DAN he becomes part of an established network exclusively dedicated to education and assisting divers.

New Members

All new members receive a "Safe Diver Kit" containing the DAN Underwater Diving Accident Manual, a wallet identification card, tank decals, and an annual subscription to Alert Diver.

Prepared Members

Each prepared member will receive worldwide diving insurance, the Safe Diver Kit, and an annual subscription to Alert Diver.

The demand for DAN's services expands each year. DAN needs your help to keep up with the increasing needs of the diving community. Your membership in DAN helps to make diving safer.

For more information about DAN's services call (919) 684-2948 extension 333, or write Divers Alert Network, Box 3823, Duke University Medical Center, Durham, NC 27710.

Points To Remember

The following is a guideline for a dive emergency plan:
1. Establish (A)irway, (B)reathing, (C)irculation.
2. Give 100 percent oxygen.
3. Contact local EMS at 911 for transport to the nearest hospital.
4. Call DAN at (919) 684-8111.

A medical diagnosis of a diving injury should not be made in the field but should be treated with standard diving first aid until the case is turned over to medical professionals.

NARCOTIC EFFECTS OF COMPRESSED AIR DIVING

(30-100 ft.) . . . . Mild impairment of performance on unpracticed tasks. Mild euphoria.

(100 ft.) . . . . Reasoning and immediate memory affected more than motor coordination and choice reactions. Delayed response to visual and auditory stimuli.

(100-165 ft.) . . . . Laughter and loquacity may be overcome by self control. Idea fixation and overconfidence. Calculation errors.

(165 ft.) . . . . Sleepiness, hallucinations, impaired judgment.

(165-230 ft.) . . . . Convivial group atmosphere. May be terror reaction in some. Talkative. Dizziness reported occasionally. Uncontrolled laughter approaching hysteria in some.

(230 ft.) . . . . Severe impairment of intellectual performance. Manual dexterity less affected.

(230-300 ft.) . . . . Gross delay in response to stimuli. Diminished concentration. Mental confusion. Increased auditory sensitivity, i.e., sounds seem louder.

(300 ft.) . . . . Stupefaction. Severe impairment of practical activity and judgment. Mental abnormalities and memory defects. Deterioration in handwriting, euphoria, hyperexcitability. Almost total loss of intellectual and perceptive faculties.

(300 ft.) . . . . Hallucinations (similar to those cuased by hallucinogenic drugs rather than alcohol).

CREDIT: Derived from Edmonds, Lowry, and Pennefather 1976.

TYPICAL TOTAL AIR DIVE DURATIONS

■ TIME IN PARENTHESES EXPRESSED AS:
(HOURS : MINUTES)

Depth, feet	15	20	30	40	50	60	80	90	100	120	150	160	200	220	250	300
190	29 MIN (:29)	51 MIN (:51)	93 MIN (1:33)	143 MIN (2:23)												
180	27 MIN (:27)	46 MIN (:46)	83 MIN (1:23)	133 MIN (2:13)	178 MIN (2:58)											
170	25 MIN (:25)	42 MIN (:42)	76 MIN (1:16)	122 MIN (2:02)	160 MIN (2:40)	213 MIN (3:33)										
160	23 MIN (:23)	37 MIN (:37)	71 MIN (1:11)	112 MIN (1:52)	149 MIN (2:29)	193 MIN (3:13)										
150	21 MIN (:21)	32 MIN (:32)	65 MIN (1:05)	100 MIN (1:40)	139 MIN (2:19)	173 MIN (2:53)	254 MIN (4:14)									
140	19 MIN (:19)	28 MIN (:28)	58 MIN (:58)	86 MIN (1:26)	126 MIN (2:06)	157 MIN (2:37)	235 MIN (3:55)									
130	18 MIN (:18)	26 MIN (:26)	53 MIN (:53)	77 MIN (1:17)	113 MIN (1:53)	146 MIN (2:26)	211 MIN (3:31)									
120	NO DECOMP	24 MIN (:24)	46 MIN (:46)	72 MIN (1:12)	98 MIN (1:38)	131 MIN (2:11)	187 MIN (3:07)	222 MIN (3:42)	250 MIN (4:10)							
110	NO DECOMP	NO DECOMP	39 MIN (:39)	65 MIN (1:05)	86 MIN (1:26)	116 MIN (1:56)	169 MIN (2:49)	198 MIN (3:18)	226 MIN (3:46)							
100	NO DECOMP	NO DECOMP	35 MIN (:35)	57 MIN (:57)	78 MIN (1:18)	99 MIN (1:39)	153 MIN (2:33)	175 MIN (2:55)	198 MIN (3:18)	253 MIN (4:13)						
90	NO DECOMP	NO DECOMP	NO DECOMP	49 MIN (:49)	70 MIN (1:10)	87 MIN (1:27)	135 MIN (2:15)	158 MIN (2:38)	177 MIN (2:57)	222 MIN (3:42)						
80	NO DECOMP	NO DECOMP	NO DECOMP	NO DECOMP	61 MIN (1:01)	78 MIN (1:18)	114 MIN (1:54)	137 MIN (2:17)	158 MIN (2:38)	194 MIN (3:14)	260 MIN (4:20)					
70	NO DECOMP	NO DECOMP	NO DECOMP	NO DECOMP	NO DECOMP	69 MIN (1:09)	99 MIN (1:39)	114 MIN (1:54)	134 MIN (2:14)	172 MIN (2:52)	221 MIN (3:41)	246 MIN (4:06)				
60	NO DECOMP	NO DECOMP	NO DECOMP	NO DECOMP	NO DECOMP	NO DECOMP	88 MIN (1:28)	105 MIN (1:45)	115 MIN (1:55)	147 MIN (2:27)	199 MIN (3:19)	209 MIN (3:29)	271 MIN (4:31)			
50	NO DECOMP	NO DECOMP	NO DECOMP	NO DECOMP	NO DECOMP	NO DECOMP	NO DECOMP	NO DECOMP	NO DECOMP	126 MIN (2:06)	172 MIN (2:52)	182 MIN (3:02)	236 MIN (3:56)	261 MIN (4:21)		
40	NO DECOMP	NO DECOMP	NO DECOMP	NO DECOMP	NO DECOMP	NO DECOMP	NO DECOMP	NO DECOMP	NO DECOMP	NO DECOMP	NO DECOMP	NO DECOMP	NO DECOMP	232 MIN (3:52)	262 MIN (4:22)	320 MIN (5:20)

Bottom Time, minutes

CREDIT: US Navy Diving Manual

Diving Safety & Medicine

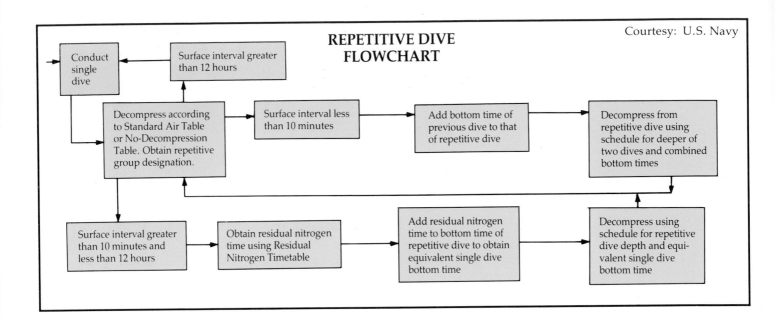

REPETITIVE DIVE
FLOWCHART

Courtesy: U.S. Navy

REPETITIVE DIVE WORKSHEET – NOAA

I. PREVIOUS DIVE:

_____ minutes

_____ feet

_____ repetitive group designation

II. SURFACE INTERVAL:

_____ hours _____ minutes on surface.

Repetitive group from I _____

New repetitive group from surface

Residual Nitrogen Timetable _____

III. RESIDUAL NITROGEN TIME:

_____ feet (depth of repetitive dive)

New repetitive group from II. _____

Residual nitrogen time from

Residual Nitrogen Timetable_____

IV. EQUIVALENT SINGLE DIVE TIME:

_____ minutes, residual nitrogen time from III.

+ _____ minutes, actual bottom time of repetitive dive.

= _____ minutes, equivalent single dive time.

V. DECOMPRESSION FOR REPETITIVE DIVES:

_____ minutes, equivalent single dive time from IV.

_____ feet, depth of repetitive dive

Decompression from (check one):
☐ Standard Air Table   ☐ No-Decompression Table
☐ Surface Table Using Oxygen   ☐ Surface Table Using Air
☐ No decompression required

Schedule used_____

Repetitive group_____

Decompression Stops:

_____ feet _____ minutes

_____ feet _____ minutes

_____ feet _____ minutes

_____ feet _____ minutes

_____ feet _____ minutes

DIVE TEAM HAWAII

"We put our best fin forward!"

Dive Team Hawaii represents the leaders in Hawaiian Island diving on the islands of Maui, Oahu and Hawaii. Our guided dives take you on a fascinating adventure into one of the world's most unique and alluring dive destinations.

A sunken shipwreck, a "forbidden island," breathtaking seascapes of volcanic formations, a high-tech submarine and waters teeming with exotic marine life, plus a clarity and brilliance only Hawaiian waters can boast!

Established in 1978, **Lahaina Divers** is dedicated to providing divers access to some of the most spectacular dive sites in and around Maui, Molokini and Lanai aboard the 43' RELIANT and 50' ENDEAVOR. Lahaina Divers' commitment to marine ecology is solidly interwoven with its proven track record for quality service. *Let us take you there in style!*

Kona Coast Divers brings you the finest in "one stop", full service dive operations with their charters, classes and dive center. Known for its great combination of high visibility, warm temperatures and smooth surface conditions, the coast of the "Big Island" of Hawaii is a true diver's paradise aboard DIVER TWO and C-K9. *Our guarantee to you is the very best diving available!*

For a truly unique diving experience, **Atlantis Reef Divers** is a must! The extraordinary adventure begins aboard the comfortable 60' EXPLORER cruising off the coast of world famous Waikiki. Entering these tropical waters you'll experience the thrill of diving Hawaii's largest sunken ship, two submerged airliners or alongside the high-tech Atlantis Submarine. *Its an experience equal to none!*

Choose **Dive Team Hawaii** for Hawaiian Island diving at its best. Please call or write for more information.

Lahaina Divers	**Kona Coast Divers**	**Atlantis Reef Divers**
710 Front Street	75-5614 Palani Road	1085 Ala Moana Blvd.
Whalers Village Mall	Kailua-Kona, HI 96740	Suite 102
Lahaina, HI 96761	1-800-KOA-DIVE	Honolulu, HI 96814
1-800-998-DIVE		1-800-554-6267

REPETITIVE DIVE TABLES

Repetitive group designation table — No-decompression limits and repetitive groups

DEPTH (feet)	NO-DECOMPRESSION LIMITS (Min.)	A	B	C	D	E	F	G	H	I	J	K	L	M	N	O
10	—	60	120	210	300	—	—	—	—	—	—	—	—	—	—	—
15	—	35	70	110	160	225	350	—	—	—	—	—	—	—	—	—
20	—	25	50	75	100	135	180	240	325	—	—	—	—	—	—	—
25	—	20	35	55	75	100	125	160	195	245	315	—	—	—	—	—
30	310	15	30	45	60	75	95	120	145	170	205	250	310	—	—	—
35	310	5	15	25	40	50	60	80	100	120	140	160	190	220	270	310
40	200	5	15	25	30	40	50	70	80	100	110	130	150	170	200	—
50	100	—	10	15	25	30	40	50	60	70	80	90	100	—	—	—
60	60	—	10	15	20	25	30	40	50	55	60	—	—	—	—	—
70	50	—	5	10	15	20	30	35	40	45	50	—	—	—	—	—
80	40	—	5	10	15	20	25	30	35	40	—	—	—	—	—	—
90	30	—	5	10	12	15	20	25	30	—	—	—	—	—	—	—
100	25	—	5	7	10	15	22	25	—	—	—	—	—	—	—	—
110	20	—	—	5	10	13	15	20	—	—	—	—	—	—	—	—
120	15	—	—	5	10	12	15	—	—	—	—	—	—	—	—	—
130	10	—	—	5	8	10	—	—	—	—	—	—	—	—	—	—
140	10	—	—	5	7	10	—	—	—	—	—	—	—	—	—	—
150	5	—	—	—	5	—	—	—	—	—	—	—	—	—	—	—
160	5	—	—	—	5	—	—	—	—	—	—	—	—	—	—	—
170	5	—	—	—	5	—	—	—	—	—	—	—	—	—	—	—
180	5	—	—	—	5	—	—	—	—	—	—	—	—	—	—	—
190	5	—	—	—	5	—	—	—	—	—	—	—	—	—	—	—

REPETITIVE GROUPS (AIR DIVES)

INSTRUCTIONS FOR USE

I. No-decompression limits:

This column shows at various depths greater than 30 feet the allowable diving times (in minutes) which permit surfacing directly at 60 feet a minute with no decompression stops. Longer exposure times require the use of the Standard Air Decompression Table (table 1–10).

II. Repetitive group designation table:

The tabulated exposure times (or bottom times) are in minutes. The times at the various depths in each vertical column are the maximum exposures during which a diver will remain within the group listed at the head of the column.

To find the repetitive group designation at surfacing for dives involving exposures up to and including the no-decompression limits: Enter the table on the exact or next greater depth than that to which exposed and select the listed exposure time exact or next greater than the actual exposure time. The repetitive group designation is indicated by the letter at the head of the vertical column where the selected exposure time is listed.

For example: A dive was to 32 feet for 45 minutes. Enter the table along the 35-foot-depth line since it is next greater than 32 feet. The table shows that since group D is left after 40 minutes' exposure and group E after 50 minutes, group E (at the head of the column where the 50-minute exposure is listed) is the proper selection.

Exposure times for depths less than 40 feet are listed only up to approximately 5 hours since this is considered to be beyond field requirements for this table.

"No decompression" limits and repetitive group designation table for "no decompression" dives.

U.S. Navy Standard Air Decompression Table

Depths 40–110 feet

DEPTH (ft)	BOTTOM TIME (min)	TIME TO FIRST STOP (min:sec)	50	40	30	20	10	TOTAL ASCENT (min:sec)	REPET GROUP
40	200	0:30					0	0:40	N
	210	0:30					2	2:40	N
	230	0:30					7	7:40	O
	250	0:30					11	11:40	O
	270	0:30					15	15:40	O
	300	0:30					19	19:40	Z
50	100	0:40					0	0:50	(*)
	110	0:40					3	3:50	L
	120	0:40					5	5:50	M
	140	0:40					10	10:50	M
	160	0:40					21	21:50	N
	180	0:40					29	29:50	O
	200	0:40					35	35:50	O
	220	0:40					40	40:50	Z
	240	0:40					47	47:50	Z
60	60	0:50					0	1:00	(*)
	70	0:50					2	3:00	K
	80	0:50					7	8:00	L
	100	0:50					14	15:00	M
	120	0:50					26	27:00	N
	140	0:50					39	40:00	O
	160	0:50					48	49:00	Z
	180	0:50					56	57:00	Z
	200	0:50				1	69	71:00	Z
70	50	1:00					0	1:10	(*)
	60	1:00					8	9:10	K
	70	1:00					14	15:10	L
	80	1:00					18	19:10	M
	90	1:00					23	24:10	N
	100	1:00					33	34:10	N
	110	1:00				2	41	44:10	O
	120	1:00				4	47	52:10	O
	130	1:00				6	52	59:10	Z
	140	1:00				8	56	65:10	Z
	150	1:00				9	61	71:10	Z
	160	1:00				13	72	86:10	Z
	170	1:00				19	79	99:10	Z
80	40	1:10					0	1:20	(*)
	50	1:10					10	11:20	K
	60	1:10					17	18:20	L
	70	1:10					23	24:20	M
	80	1:10				2	31	34:20	N
	90	1:10				7	39	47:20	N
	100	1:10				11	46	58:20	O
	110	1:10				13	53	67:20	O
	120	1:10				17	56	74:20	Z
	130	1:10				19	63	83:20	Z
	140	1:10				26	69	96:20	Z
	150	1:10				32	77	110:20	Z
90	30	1:30					0	1:40	(*)
	40	1:20					7	8:30	K
	50	1:20					18	19:30	L
	60	1:20					25	26:30	M
	70	1:20				7	30	38:30	N
	80	1:20				13	40	54:30	N
	90	1:20				18	48	67:30	O
	100	1:20				21	54	76:30	Z
	110	1:20				24	61	86:30	Z
	120	1:20				32	68	101:30	Z
	130	1:20				36	74	116:30	Z
100	25	1:40					0	1:50	(*)
	30	1:30					3	4:40	H
	40	1:30					15	16:40	K
	50	1:30				2	24	27:40	L
	60	1:30				9	28	38:40	N
	70	1:20			2	17	39	59:40	O
	80	1:20			7	23	48	79:40	O
	90	1:20			12	23	57	93:40	Z
	100	1:20			15	30	64	110:40	Z
	110	1:20		2	19	33	74	129:40	Z
	120	1:20		6	21	37	80	145:40	Z
110	20	1:50					0	2:00	(*)
	25	1:40					3	4:50	H
	30	1:40					7	8:50	J
	40	1:30				2	21	24:50	L
	50	1:30			8	23	35	55:50	N?
	60	1:30			18	23	53	73:50	O
	70	1:20		1	23	24	62	88:50	Z
	80	1:20		7	23	33	72	107:50	Z
	90	1:20		12	30	33	72	147:50	Z
	100	1:20		15	37	37	84	183:50	Z

Depths 120–190 feet

DEPTH (ft)	BOTTOM TIME (min)	TIME TO FIRST STOP (min:sec)	50	40	30	20	10	TOTAL ASCENT (min:sec)	REPET GROUP
120	15	1:50					0	2:00	(*)
	20	1:50					2	4:00	H
	25	1:50					6	8:00	I
	30	1:50					14	16:00	J
	40	1:50				5	25	32:00	L
	50	1:40			2	15	31	50:00	M
	60	1:40			9	22	39	72:00	N
	80	1:30		3	16	24	61	106:00	O
	100	1:30		10	23	34	74	143:00	Z
	120	1:30		18	23	45	80	168:00	Z
130	10	2:00					0	2:10	(*)
	15	2:00					1	3:10	F
	20	2:00					4	6:10	H
	25	2:00					10	12:10	J
	30	2:00				3	18	23:10	M
	40	1:50				10	25	37:10	N
	50	1:50			3	21	37	63:10	O
	60	1:50			9	23	52	86:10	Z
	70	1:40		2	19	26	61	103:10	Z
	80	1:40		10	19	37	72	131:10	Z
	90	1:30	3	11	19	45	80	154:10	Z
140	10	2:10					0	2:20	(*)
	15	2:10					2	4:20	G
	20	2:10					6	8:20	I
	25	2:00				2	14	18:20	J
	30	2:00				5	21	28:20	K
	40	2:00			2	16	26	46:20	N
	50	1:50			6	24	44	76:20	O
	60	1:50			16	23	56	97:20	Z
	70	1:50		4	19	32	68	125:20	Z
	80	1:40		10	23	41	79	155:20	Z
150	5	2:20					0	2:30	C
	10	2:20					1	3:30	E
	15	2:20					3	5:30	G
	20	2:20				2	7	11:30	H
	25	2:10				3	17	22:30	K
	30	2:10			2	8	24	36:30	L
	40	2:10			5	19	33	59:30	N
	50	2:00		2	12	23	51	90:30	O
	60	2:00		5	19	26	62	114:30	Z
	70	1:50	2	8	23	39	75	149:30	Z
	80	1:50	2	17	19	50	84	174:30	Z
160	5	2:30					0	2:40	D
	10	2:30					2	4:40	F
	15	2:30					5	7:40	H
	20	2:20				2	11	15:40	J
	25	2:20				7	20	29:40	K
	30	2:20			4	13	26	45:40	M
	40	2:10		2	10	23	39	76:40	N
	50	2:10		9	17	19	50	97:40	Z
	60	2:00	1	17	19	39	69	147:40	Z
	70	2:00	1	17	22	44	86	173:40	Z
170	5	2:40					0	2:50	D
	10	2:40					3	6:00	F
	15	2:30				2	5	9:50	H
	20	2:30				4	15	21:50	J
	25	2:30			2	7	23	34:50	L
	30	2:20			4	13	26	45:50	M
	40	2:20		3	10	24	43	80:50	N
	50	2:10		9	19	23	58	112:50	O
	60	2:10	2	14	23	34	72	155:50	Z
	70	2:00	8	17	23	44	83	183:50	Z
180	5	2:50					0	3:00	D
	10	2:50					3	6:00	F
	15	2:40				3	6	12:00	H
	20	2:40				5	17	24:00	J
	25	2:40			3	10	24	40:00	L
	30	2:30		2	6	17	27	53:00	M
	40	2:30		6	14	23	50	84:00	N
	50	2:20	2	9	19	30	65	128:00	O
	60	2:20	5	16	19	44	81	168:00	Z
190	5	3:00					0	3:10	D
	10	2:50				1	3	7:10	G
	15	2:50				4	7	14:10	H
	20	2:50			2	6	14	25:10	J
	25	2:50			5	11	25	44:10	L
	30	2:40		1	8	19	32	63:10	M
	40	2:30	3	8	14	23	55	103:10	N
	50	2:30	4	13	22	33	72	147:10	O
	60	2:20	10	17	19	50	84	183:10	Z

U.S. Navy Standard Air Decompression Table